How to Click with EVERYONE EVERY TIME

DB65206231

DISCOVER THE **10** SECRETS TO:

→ Making People Like You

→ Having Great Conversations Effortlessly

→ Being a "Contagiously" Appealing Person with Everyone

DAVID A. RICH

AMERICA'S #1 EXPERT ON PERSUASION AND MOTIVATION

How to Click with Everyone Every Time

How to Click with Everyone Every Time

David A. Rich

McGraw-Hill
New York   Chicago   San Francisco   Lisbon
London   Madrid   Mexico City   Milan   New Delhi
San Juan   Seoul   Singapore   Sydney   Toronto

The McGraw·Hill Companies

1 2 3 4 5 6 7 8 9 0   AGM/AGM   0 9 8 7 6 5 4

ISBN 0-07-141847-4

McGraw-Hill books are available at special quantity discounts to use as premiums and sales promotions, or for use in corporate training programs. For more information, please write to the Director of Special Sales, Professional Publishing, McGraw-Hill, Two Penn Plaza, New York, NY 10121-2298. Or contact your local bookstore.

Library of Congress Cataloging-in-Publication Data

Rich, David (David A.)
    How to click with everyone every time / by David Rich.
        p. cm.
    ISBN 0-07-141847-4 (alk. paper)
        1. Customer relations. 2. Interpersonal attraction. 3. Success in business.
    I. Title.

HF5415.5.R594   2003
650.1'3–dc22   2003018800

This book is printed on recycled, acid-free paper containing a minimum of 50% recycled, de-inked fiber.

Special thanks to Sean Lyden, a gentleman I've never met, but without whom this book would never have happened.

Contents

Preface

Did you clash with someone recently, or feel ignored or shut down? Or perhaps you bought this book because you simply want to connect more easily and naturally with others?

You are not alone. In a time-starved, increasingly transient world where fewer people have an extended set of family and friends, we hunger for healthier ways to connect.

Sit back and get comfortable. With Will Rogers—like contagious warmth, David pulls you into his world to show you how to click.

You are in for a treat. By the time you put this book down, you will feel like his friend. Why? Because he practices what he preaches—he makes it fun and fascinating to learn.

From his teen years in the unexpected job as a home health aide to his rapid rise as a popular public speaker, David has been on a journey. He's been searching for the lessons that would not only make him successful but also enable him to savor his life *with others*.

Those lessons appeared, of course, through the people he's met along the way. And you get the opportunity to meet them.

- A Realtor, seeking to stand out from the crowd of competitors, considers evoking his childhood passion for comic book heroes to proclaim that same passion for serving his clients ("If I can't move your house, nobody can!") But what does he ultimately decide to do, and why?

- A young quadriplegic, deserted by his wife who took two of their three children with her, demonstrates an unexpected quality that's remained a vivid memory since David met him as a teenager.

- A beloved woman speaker gently asks David a life-changing question. How would you answer?

Welcome to the "rich" world of colorful characters who come alive in the following pages. They can serve as your memory anchors so that when you rise up from your seat and return to your life, you will remember the right one to click in your next encounter.

How do you warm up that grumpy person serving you, reignite the passion in a coworker who feels stale or dispirited? How can you pull someone closer?

Discover the answers in David's 10 very human qualities for clicking with others. These stories and lessons will give you the fuel to find your way more easily with others. Through the strong, affirming attitude he exudes, David brings out others' better side, and so can you.

For work, family, friends, or those brief encounters with strangers, Rich is offering you not only lessons, but also a life philosophy and your handy tool to live life more fully—*with others.*

As David writes, "Courage takes an act." Your first courageous act is in taking this step to learn how you, too, can cultivate the genuine, enduring relationships that give life so much more meaning.

Here's to your clicking!

Kare Anderson, author of LikeABILITY (an e-book),
Getting What You Want, Resolving Conflict Sooner,
Walk Your Talk: Grow Your Business FasterThrough
Successful Cross-Promotional Partnerships, and
Beauty Inside Out: 80 Ways to Becoming
Positively Unforgettable

Introduction

Have you stopped to ponder why it is that we "click" with some people and "clash" with others? It is truly one of life's great questions. It could be ranked right up there with the chicken and the egg or the meaning of life, questions with no definitive answer. Yet it is undeniable that some people seem to possess that intangible quality that serves to draw people to them. We've witnessed people who naturally and effortlessly are able to click with people almost instantly.

I sometimes think of people who click easily with others as people who are "contagious." They possess the qualities that others are drawn to. They are infectious, but not in the negative, stay away from me way, but in a positive, compelling way. It's like a human gravitational pull.

People who are good at clicking with others do not come in one shape or size. They are both male and female, of all races, nationalities, cultures, professions, and educational levels. Clickers, (as I'll refer to them throughout this book), can be found everywhere, and at the same time, can also be found nowhere. Clicking defies logic. It goes way beyond common interests or physical attraction. People you'd think you would or should click with, you don't, while with others, in which you have nothing in common, you click. It can be both mind-boggling and frustrating.

Yet the people who seem to have the ability to contagiously and effortlessly click are the envy of their professions. Doctors who click, in addition to being good doctors, of course, are loved by patients and even thought of as part of the family. Teachers who click are fought over by parents wanting their kids to be in their classrooms. Company owners who click have no trouble finding good people, and turnover is almost nonexistent. Pastors who click have the biggest congregations. You get the picture. These people may not be the best or brightest, but they understand the importance of connecting with others, and in the end, that's what counts the most.

It's extremely hard to definitively pin down what makes someone click because it is not always logical. Sometimes it's obvious, other times it's not. There are no formulas or flow charts. Clicking is highly emotional and is the sum of many factors at play in any given situation. The sum of the parts does not come close to the sum of the whole. People have tried to master one element of clicking, or even several, but in the absence of all the parts, it falls short. It comes across insincere and manipulative. We've all encountered people who are trying their best to build rapport, but the more they try, the more they fail. Clicking must be natural or it isn't clicking at all. You might not always be aware of clicking when it's happening, and the same holds true when you're not. Rarely will someone admit that you just don't click. Someone is much more likely to make up some hollow reason to avoid you rather than confess the lack of clicking.

It's also impossible to click if you've simply mastered a technique or two. You click not just because you know how, but rather because you are "click-able." In other words, you are contagious. It's simply who you are. Forrest Gump coined the popular phrase, "Stupid is as stupid does." When it comes to clicking, it's the other way around. Clicking does as clicking is. In other words, you'll click if you are "click-able," not just because you've learned a few tricks of the trade. Although a few tricks can't hurt. I'll talk about both the inward and the outward qualities that contribute to genuine rapport.

To that end, *How to Click with Everyone Every Time* is not just a "how to" book, but rather a "how to become" book. It picks up where Dale Carnegie's classic book, *How to Win Friends and Influence People* left off. It's about developing the qualities that attract people and circumstances to you like a magnet, or in Carnegie's words, like bees to honey. Fellow speaker Charlie "Tremendous" Jones is known to say that you'll be exactly the same person you are today with the exception of two things: the books you read and the people you meet. Well, I contend that reading this book will help with the people you meet, thus killing both birds with one book!

The quality of a person's life is directly linked to the quality of their relationships, and I will tackle both. We'll explore the 10 qualities, or contagions, that if developed, can enhance your relationships and change your life. By becoming a clicker, you will take the leap from merely interacting to being irresistible. You will be contagious. You will not only talk the talk, but walk the walk as well. In this book, we will look at 10 external qualities that persuade and influence people as well as the corresponding internal qualities that make your interactions sincere and authentic.

Socrates once said, "May the outward man and the inward man be as one." That is the journey of the people who endeavor to click, to be the same person on the inside that they appear to be on the outside. It's not a common feat. Some books tackle the outer man, some the inner, but they're incomplete. Both parts are needed if you intend to click with everyone every time.

So are you ready? We'll explore both the inner and outer qualities that are necessary to clicking and overall success and happiness. There are 10 in all. I call them "contagions." I know it's hard to believe, but coincidentally, all 10 qualities also begin with the letter C. Well, what did you expect with a book about "Clicking?"

How to Click with
Everyone Every Time

1

The Missing Link

Clicking is at the heart of every transaction and interaction. Whether it is in business or pleasure, your ability to click with others is the defining factor in determining the quality of that interaction. Clicking happens, or doesn't happen, in seconds. I've been known, and I'll bet you have too, to hang up the phone on customer service people simply because something in the sound of their voices didn't click with me. Conversely, there have been times when I went out of my way to do business with someone because we clicked.

Clicking happens at rates undetectable to the conscious mind. Various studies put the timing of a first impression between 2 and 12 seconds. I don't know how that can ever be measured, but my own experience says it is true. First impressions are indeed a part of and crucial to clicking, but clicking goes well past a first impression.

Clicking is the intangible ability to connect with someone instantly and naturally. Clicking is a contagious quality that others cannot immediately define. It's that person you just love to be around. You can't really explain it, but you're drawn to them. You admire them, but not in a physical, superficial way, but in a genuine, heartfelt way. It's difficult to explain, but you know when you click with some-one. But then, of course, there's the person you avoid at every cost. The reason might be just as inexplicable. You don't have any con-scious cause to dislike them. It's just a gut feeling. You simply don't click.

Wouldn't it be an awesome thing if there were a vitamin we could take that would instantly enable us to click with every person we meet? Every day, there's a new study supporting the use of this vitamin or that vitamin. Why not isolate the clicking gene? It could be sold on the black market, or be given away like the flu shot to those who need it the most. That would be great. Or would it? Besides the obvious; (there'd be no need for this book), if clicking were commonplace then it wouldn't be as special when it happens. Clicking is magical largely because we know what it's like to not click. It's kind of like good and evil. We know good because we know evil and vice versa.

Clicking is rare, and that's a good thing. I often call it the miss-ing link. It's what's missing in most self-help programs and books. It's ignored at the corporate level. It's dismissed as something you either have or don't. It's viewed as a soft skill. The truth of the mat-ter is it's as hard a skill as any. Clicking is where the rubber meets the road. It's the foundation of dealing with people. We don't spend the time on it because we don't understand it, and certainly don't believe it can be created without being fake or manipulative. There are plenty of books on creating a false kind of rapport. But that's not what I'm tackling in this book. I'm talking about clicking from the inside out, not the other way around.

Clicking is as much an adjective as it is a verb. It's an inner quality that shines through the body and eyes. If you ever saw Ingrid Bergman in Casablanca you know what I'm talking about. It's more about who you are than what you do. You click by first becoming "click-able." Clicking becomes natural and automatic when you pos-sess and develop the qualities of clicking, rather than relying on forced skills or available tools. You're probably asking yourself what's the difference. The difference is subtle, but huge. It's the missing link in relationships. Let me explain.

TRAINING VERSUS EDUCATION

Customer service and emphasis on building a true rapport in corporate America has been on a downward spiral for the past 20 years, and there are two major causes. The first lies in the difference between training and education. Companies spend hundreds of millions of dollars each year training their employees. This is a good thing. There's an old saying by Mark Twain that captures the importance of training. He said, "It is better to train your people and lose them than to not train them and keep them."

Certainly, training is crucial to survival these days, but training falls short of the mark. It's like an elevator stopping two feet above the floor level. You're in the right vicinity, but not quite there. Training gives people the how, where, and when. Education gives them the why. A perfect example of the chasm between training and education is the experience I had at a fast-food restaurant one afternoon. I had just finished ordering and like many before, the gal inside thanked me for coming. Unlike hundreds of times before (I guess I was in an unusually jovial mood), I stuck my head back out of my car window and thanked her for taking my order. Perhaps something in her voice triggered my unexplained moment of politeness. Before I had a chance to put my car in gear to drive forward, she came back on the intercom, almost flustered, and thanked me again. This time I'm confused. Did she not hear my acknowledgment of her first thank you? Is she flirting with me? Is she in some way mocking me? Worse yet, maybe I'm on *Candid Camera*. It's not like me to not know how to respond, but I was speechless. But then, like a beacon of revelation, it hit me what was going on. I leaned back out of my window and thanked her again for taking my order. I waited for her next move to confirm my hunch. Sure enough, she came back on the intercom, albeit a bit more forcefully this time, and thanked me a third time for coming. Without hesitating this time, she begged me to please pull forward. Which I did, but gosh knows I might still be there if I had dared to respond again. She was trained to have the last word. She was probably instructed to end every exchange with a thank you, and that's precisely what she did. She performed her duties perfectly.

On yet another occasion, I was walking up to a sporting goods store when I met with the store greeter. She had seen me coming and opened the door for me, and as I stepped inside, she welcomed me to the store. I was impressed. I had certainly been greeted before, but never in a retail store had someone opened the door for me. So I stopped and genuinely expressed my gratitude. Her response is something I'll never forget. She nodded reluctantly and said, "I have to; it's my job." I stood stunned at her confession. I wanted to say, "Oh, so if it weren't your job, you'd have let the door hit me in the you know what." But I held my tongue. Some might suggest that I should have been grateful that she did her job. Perhaps. But if we expect to click, we need to be nice to people not because it's our job, but because it's who we are. She had the external skills down pat, but lacked the internal qualities at that moment to leave a positive impression.

These examples are but a couple of many stories I could share to make my point about training versus education. In both of these examples, the people I encountered were trained, and trained well. They were efficient in doing their jobs. In fact, if I were their manager evaluating their performances, I might have to give each a thumbs-up. They did as they were trained to do. However, neither passed the clicking test. Neither was positively contagious. They were just the opposite. Despite their efficiency, they left me with negative impressions. They were trained, but not educated. They knew what to do; they just didn't know why they were doing it or what effect their actions would have on customers.

Training tells people what to do, when to do it, and how to do it. Education, however, tells them why. Training is a necessary evil, but it's not the complete puzzle. Taking the extra step to explain to someone "why" to do something is empowering and will enable that person to click. Too often, companies focus too hard on efficiency and production at the expense of clicking and rapport. In other words, they're good at training, but not at educating.

So, is efficiency even important? Of course, but it's a given. In other words, in these competitive times, efficiency is essential just to stay in business. It's the ante simply to stay in the poker game. It doesn't mean you'll win. If you want to do more than just survive, if you want to thrive, you must be good at the clicking game as well. It's the missing link.

The other explanation as to why customer service (and subsequently, clicking), has slipped a few notches is that it is often not seen as a learned skill. Too often, customer service is used as an entry-level position or a place just to do some time before graduating to a more skillful position. Customer service, like clicking, is reduced to the concept of "just be friendly." Very few people recognize the art and skill behind genuine rapport. Through the years, if I had a dollar for every client who referred to clicking and building rapport as a soft skill, I'd be rich. Well, besides just having the name. There might be many explanations for this, but one has to be the perceived lack of correlation to the bottom line. Making a sale, balancing the books, entering data, packaging goods, these add to the bottom line, but smiling at a customer, taking an extra minute to listen, or going out of your way to be nice, well, these are soft skills. How unfortunate. People, of course, want to "just be friendly," but unless they understand the dynamics of interpersonal communication, even being friendly can fall short of real and lasting rapport.

The hard truth is more businesses go out of business because of these so-called soft skills than any other reason. The trouble is, I can't prove it. Data can't capture this information. When a product is defective, we have no problem letting someone know. After all, it's not personal; it's just a defective product. However, when it's a clicking issue (or rather lack of clicking issue), we rarely fess up. It's highly personal. Can you remember a time when you went into a store you swore you'd never go back to, just to tell them the reason for your absence is that you didn't like someone? Probably not. We'd probably be more likely to make up some story to explain our absence rather than admit that we just didn't click with someone. To make matters worse, we sometimes aren't even aware that we didn't click. Why get personal if we don't have to? In business, it's called the "Eureka Factor." The "Eureka Factor" says that people buy based on subjective experience, but they validate it with logic. In plainer English, it means we make decisions based on emotion, but explain and justify our decisions with fact and logic. The same dynamic applies to clicking. When there isn't a clicking connection, we often rationalize with subjective reasoning. We say things like "The price wasn't right" or "They didn't have the right item" when the real reason for our discontent is purely emotional and personal. We didn't click. Sometimes we know it, and other times, we don't . We often know right away when we click, but it isn't as obvious when we don't, and even then, we rarely admit it.

THE IMPACT OF TECHNOLOGY

And then, there's technology. Technology is definitely a mixed bag. On one hand, it is life changing. What did we ever do without cell phones or emails? I've learned more about the lives of strangers (more than I really wanted to know) inadvertently by overhearing cell phone conversations, than I know about some of my neighbors. I'm just waiting for books to be written on cell phone etiquette. Maybe they're out already. When I am in the position of having to be subjected to someone's personal conversation, I'm usually overcome by conflicting thoughts. First, guilt over finding myself captivated by some of my newly acquired data, and the other is regret over not knowing more about the people I really care about. Why don't I know more about my neighbors, coworkers, and friends? When was the last time I went out of my way to have lunch with my mom or sisters? This book was perhaps spawned by some of that regret. If I could contribute something to be part of the solution rather than part of the problem, then that's a good thing.

But don't get me wrong. I'm not labeling technology as a problem per se. I rely on the conveniences of modern technology as much as anyone. The problem lies in how we use it. Technology is now used to replace real relationships rather than enhance them. My emphasis is on the word real. We think we're clicking when we send an email or leave a voice mail, but in many cases, just the opposite is true. About 10 years ago, there was a commercial for United Airlines that started with the sales manager walking into a meeting by announcing that they had just lost their oldest account. He went on to say that business relationships had become a fax and a message left on someone's machine. He proceeded to hand out airline tickets to each sales rep, exhorting them to get face to face with each and every customer again. He then turned to walk out of the room and one of the reps asked where he was going; he replied he was going to see their old friend again. I just love that commercial. It was truly prophetic.

Of course, emails have replaced faxes and voice mail has replaced answering machines, but the United Airlines commercial was right on. I even catch myself sometimes hoping to get someone's voice mail just to avoid personal contact. After all, I just want to say one thing. I'm busy, right? Wrong. Somehow we've all gotten busier, and while emails and voice mails make communication easier and more convenient, they have damaged real rapport. I call it the "busy syndrome." We are as busy as we think we are. If we think we are busy, we will be busy. If our minds are not at peace, even in the midst of a lot of activity, we will act panicked and hurried. We need to train our minds to be calm. This is easier said than done, but it speaks to the heart of clicking. I even go as far as to counsel sales people to only leave messages on someone's voice mail as an absolute last resort. The goal, after all, is not merely to make contact, but to make a connection, and that can only be done face to face, or at least, voice to voice.

To make real connections and click is as much an attitude as it is an action. We need to first *want* to click, and that perhaps requires a shift in priorities. Because of technology, we know more people in terms of sheer numbers than our grandparents did, but the depths of our relationships are much more shallow. Real is knowing someone's heart, not just knowing their email address. Real is knowing their hopes and aspirations for the future, not just how much their account is worth. Harvey MacKay, owner of MacKay Envelope Company and author of *How to Swim with the Sharks without Being Eaten Alive*, recognized this two decades ago. He invented what has since been called the "MacKay 66." It is 66 questions that his company asks their customers. Not all at one time, just a few here and there. Questions like "Are they married? When is their birthday? and Do they have a favorite baseball team?" Questions show the customer that the company cares and is interested in building a real relationship. They then customized their software program to accommodate the data so they could retrieve it when necessary. How powerful do you think it is to be able to say "happy birthday" to a customer without having to be reminded? The answer, of course, is very. Real clicking requires a commitment to doing it. It means taking the extra minute to say hello when all you really wanted to do is leave a message. Use technology, but the goal should be to click, not just an easy escape. Even emails that once were personal have fallen victim to the "busy" syndrome." Instead of taking the extra time to build rapport, we abbreviate words and phrases. The overwhelming majority of my dozens of emails a day are less than 10 words. Quick, yes. Efficient? Perhaps. Is it ideal for clicking? No.

We've already talked about how efficiency and clicking are not synonymous. Clicking takes a commitment to want to do so, and it takes time and effort. I relate it to the age-old argument about quality time versus quantity. I believe it's the people who think they're "too busy" that say quality time is what counts. I have another view. Many psychologists and therapists now conclude that quality time is nice, but the amount of time spent with someone is much more influential.

A daily chat around a dinner table is better than a weekly trip to the zoo. This concept hit home personally a few months ago when we were hit with a once-in-a-lifetime ice storm. We lost power for four days. When the power first went out, everyone was in separate rooms either watching TV, on the phone, or on a computer. Within seconds, we were all in the same room, talking, and playing checkers. We spent the better part of the next four days together and have since joked that we're sorry the lights came back on. We were having clicking on all cylinders. Could we have done so if the power hadn't gone off? Yes. But we wouldn't have. We were busy enjoying technology, minding our own business, and not thinking twice about it.

Every technological advance is one step forward for convenience, but one step back for relationships. We're living in very disloyal times. Customers are less loyal than at any point in time. They have more choices than ever before. My grandfather went to the same barber his entire life. He didn't always get a good haircut, but he accepted it. He and his barber were friends. They exchanged a hug and countless stories every time they saw each other. A trip to the barbershop was an event to my grandfather, not just an item on a long to-do list. Today, if we don't like the haircut, we find another place to go. Within a five-mile radius of my house are nine places to get a haircut. There are eight grocery stores, 10 banks, and more than a dozen dry cleaners. Most people go where they can get a deal, or where it's quick and convenient. Clicking rarely enters the equation. It's the missing link.

There are many things that separate human beings from the animal kingdom, but one of the biggies is that we need each other. People need other people. Our world, despite all the technological advances and modern conveniences, is becoming more disconnected every day. Increasingly, more and more people are yearning for deeper and better relationships. Churches, coffee shops, and Internet chat rooms are filled with people craving to fill the voids left by shallow relationships. All that can change in an instant. The missing link can be found. It takes two things, and both are free of charge: desire and discipline. It takes an inner desire and outward discipline to do the little things necessary to click. Where there's a will, there's a way. Regardless of gender, occupation, race, or social status, you can be a better clicker. There's no more rewarding endeavor than to improve one's life by improving the quality and quantity of one's relationships. By becoming a better and more natural "clicker," you will see dividends in almost every aspect of your life.

Clicking affects everything, and to that end, we'll explore not only the qualities that can make someone a better clicker, but the related fruits of clicking, such as success, happiness, achievement, and peace of mind. In the end, you might not have actually clicked with every single person you've ever come in contact with, but attempting to will have made all the difference in the world. British philosopher John Ruskin once said, "The highest reward for a person's toil is not what they get for it, but what they become by it." Clicking is not only about getting better relationships; it's also about becoming a better person. It's the marriage of success with others and success in life itself. The more you click with yourself and in life, the more you'll click with others. It's the ultimate success journey. So I guess congratulations are in order; you've already taken the first step!

2

The Case for Contagions

The world is full of clickers. Contagious people are found in business, politics, religion, entertainment, and sports. They come from all walks of life and from every conceivable background. There's no prerequisite for being good at clicking with people, but those who have it are unmistakable. The magnetic pull of contagiousness is hard to disguise or subdue; it comes out even when that person might be trying to go unnoticed. Let me give you a few examples.

I'll never forget the woman who picked me up at the Raleigh airport a few years back. I know that sounds suspicious, but I was traveling to speak at Pinehurst, the legendary golf community in North Carolina, and she was Pinehurst's van driver. I was picked up around 9:00 PM and was completely wiped out. I know it seems out of character for a person who makes his living speaking, but I was in the mood for small talk. After a few minutes of utter silence, I asked her to tell me about Pinehurst. I had heard about it, but this was my first visit, and besides, I couldn't take the quiet any longer. No sooner had the request left my mouth than she turned to me and almost seemed to glow in the dark. Her face lit up as she informed me that

Pinehurst was like "no other place on Earth." She described it in great detail, glowing as if she were a kid on her way to Disney World for the first time.

Her enthusiasm was contagious. Despite being tired and weary at the end of a long day, I was now truly eager to see this place for myself. We talked about the weather, life, jobs, and even politics for the rest of the ride to Pinehurst. We truly clicked.

I've told that story countless times in my presentations and have had time to analyze what happened. Contagious behaviors lead to clicking. Her energy and excitement lured me into a conversation I otherwise would not have had. She wasn't acting or playing the part of a good host. She was sincere and I knew it. Her deep conviction for Pinehurst served as a contagion to connect with me.

Another example of contagiousness leading to clicking occurred during a family trip to the Hyatt Grand Cypress hotel in Orlando. I had the privilege of speaking to their staff while I was there. At that meeting I met their bartender, Bob. He quickly gave me his card, and upon reading it I realized he was much more than a bartender. He was a "Mixologist." He explained to me that anyone could make a drink, but only a mixologist could make a masterpiece. He even had several original mixes. I'd share them but I was sworn to secrecy, but if you're ever in Orlando, I'm sure he'd love a visit. It was clear to me that this was not just a job to him. He had found a calling. His commitment to his craft was contagious, even though I don't drink. He also knew that, but it didn't matter. He wasn't selling anything, and I wasn't buying. He simply enjoys meeting new people and spreading the gospel of drink technology. I was impressed and have since sung his praises to many people. We clicked because he was sincere, and that has made a lasting impression.

Contagions are to clicking what drink mixes are to the finished product. In and of themselves, there is no magic. But in the right hands, with the right motives, mixed together with the right ingredients, they have powerful effects.

American history, business, and politics are filled with examples of contagious people. People who knew how to click and took full advantage of it include Ronald Reagan, Harry Truman, Rudy Guiliani, Oprah Winfrey, and Julia Roberts. Each possessed different contagions, but the end result was a bond that is enviable and undeniable. Ronald Reagan was one of most cheerful and optimistic presidents in history. His sense of humor and quick wit became his trademark, and probably was the major contributor to his re-election in 1984. Harry Truman was a no-nonsense kind of guy. His genuineness is legendary, and his down-to-earth demeanor allowed him to click with the American people. Rudy Guiliani's courage was the source behind his ability to click. In the face of disaster, he showed the inner strength and resolve to lead by example, and much of the nation found that to be contagious. Oprah Winfrey is a master communicator. Her ability to connect with her eyes and voice is unmatched in entertainment today. Each show is like a graduate-level course in building rapport and dealing with people. Dale Carnegie would be proud. Julia Roberts is a wide-eyed actress that makes me smile just thinking of her. Her sense of wonder and curiosity are like no one else I know, at least on screen anyway. She radiates these qualities, and that draws the audience to her. She's an on-camera clicker. There are many more examples of people with contagious qualities that click. Bill O'Reilly, love him or hate him, clicks because of his candor and conviction, Colin Powell exudes confidence and competency, I could go on and on. People who click seem to attract attention and success even if they are not actively pursuing it. It finds them. They were just being themselves, but they have an uncanny ability to be at the right place at the right time.

SYNCHRONICITY

I don't believe in fate, but I do believe in something called synchronicity. There have been many books written on this subject that define it far better than me, but I define synchronicity as the perfect assembly of people, places, circumstance, and time. It's being alive and aware of people and circumstances that have been placed in your path. Everything happens for a reason, and if you want to click with more people, you better be open and in tune to your surroundings.

More often than not, people who are contagious find themselves in moments of magical synchronicity. Synchronicity intersects with clicking on two levels. First, people who are good at clicking experience more frequent and more meaningful moments of synchronicity, and then secondly, they interpret those events differently than those who don't click. Let me illustrate. In his magnificent book, *The Tipping Point*, Malcolm Gladwell chronicles the story of Paul Revere, the man who rode through the countryside of Massachusetts on the evening of April 18, 1775 warning people of the impending attack by British soldiers. Paul Revere became famous. His story is told in history classes throughout the country. But what is incredible about Paul Revere's ride is why he had the impact he had. Gladwell writes about another patriot by the name of William Dawes, who set out on the same night, with the same message, and covered as many miles as Revere, albeit a different course. There was yet a third man, Samuel Prescott, who made the ride through the Massachusetts countryside that evening. Isn't it curious that we know Paul Revere, while Dawes and Prescott are footnotes in American history books? History tells us that the message of the "other" two men simply did not take root, and in the cities that they rode through, there were overwhelming victories for the British.

Gladwell comes to the conclusion that "William Dawes was just an ordinary man," while Paul Revere was a "maven." He describes a maven as "one who accumulates knowledge," but I'll go a step further. Paul Revere knew how to click. He was an instrument of synchronicity because of his contagiousness. He no doubt suffered similar obstacles in his ride, as did Dawes, yet Revere was successful and Dawes was not. I'm sure William Dawes was a decent man, and successful in his own right, but people, such as Revere, who know how to connect with others have an unfair advantage over those who don't. Revere's ride was special because he clicked, even though he didn't realize it at the time.

Contagious people also interpret those moments of synchronicity differently. They recognize that people are woven together for a purpose, and they don't try to explain that, they just accept it. In turn, they don't lament over unfortunate circumstances, they learn from them and move on. By and large, they are optimists who are thankful for their half glass of water instead of theorizing on why there isn't more. This outlook, which I'll go into in more detail in a later chapter, allows them to capitalize on opportunistic, synchronistic moments. They look for the good instead of the bad.

One such story of having the right perspective took place in the mid-nineteenth century. There was a young printer in Springfield, Massachusetts, who thought that he had just stumbled onto his ticket to fortune. He had released a print of a popular new presidential candidate by the name of Abraham Lincoln. It quickly became a hot selling commodity. Meanwhile, 11-year-old Grace Bedell of Westfield, New York, sent a letter to Lincoln suggesting he would look wiser if he grew a beard. Lincoln agreed, however, it didn't take long before sales of the beardless Lincoln ground to a halt. The young printer, disappointed by this unforeseen twist, had to do something to keep his print shop open. Hoping to just make enough money to survive until another print started selling, he began selling a children's game he had invented a few years earlier. The printer's name was Milton Bradley and his game was called, "The Checkered Game of Life," a name he came up with one night while pondering his next move. He saw life as being sometimes up and sometimes down, but always exciting and worth living. Life became a best-selling board game, and his company one of the most successful publishers of games in American history. The moral of the story is that Milton Bradley did not view his unfortunate turn of events (Lincoln growing a beard) as fatal. He saw it as part of life, accepted it, and moved on to something else. Too often the story goes the other way. We finally think we've gotten that big break and then suddenly something happens to pull the rug out from under us, and we give up. You've heard the saying, "When life gives you lemons, make lemonade!" That's exactly what Milton Bradley did, and he typifies the spirit of contagious people. People like to be around people who see the glass as half full instead of half empty, and your greatest opportunities often hinge on that interpretation.

The same dynamic is true for businesses as well as individuals. Most businesses reach a crossroad that ultimately determines their future. One road leads to prosperity, the other to perpetual scratching and clawing. That crossroad is usually found at the point where price and value intersect.

Imagine two parallel lines on a piece of paper; one represents the price tag, the other value. The optimal scenario has the value line stay on top and maintain a constant spacing to that of the price line. If the gap continues to widen with value ahead of price, then businesses suffer because they are selling their products or services for too little, and this will create significant supply-and-demand challenges. If the gap lessens and price is gaining on value, this means that the product or service has failed to stay fresh and has become increasingly susceptible to competition. This process is often referred to as "commoditization." This occurs when the space between value and price is so diminished that the marketplace no longer sees the true worth and value of the item. It's happened to paper clips, toothpaste, and cell phones. Commoditization is happening in almost every industry across the board. Consumers become more sophisticated and have access to more information and choices than ever before. They demand better prices or else they'll take their business elsewhere. Consumers pushed the price line toward value, and businesses, for the most part, weren't able to keep pace by raising the value line. At some point, the value and price lines might even intersect, with price moving above value.

This is a pivotal moment. One of two things can happen. The obvious is extinction. This is precisely what happened to vinyl records. Value sunk below price due mainly to the emergence of CD technology. Vinyl records were no longer worth their price. However, something else can happen when price rises above value and is the exact opposite of extinction. It is distinction. This is when the brand becomes so desired the public will pay almost anything for it. There are two categories of distinction, one is based on hollow value, and the other is real.

I've witnessed the hollow value phenomenon many times. The first was as a kid with pet rocks and glass balls tied together on a string known as "clackers." I had to have both. It was the "in" thing to do. I remember my mother trying in vain to talk me out of them. "It's just a rock," she pleaded. What do you think the markup of pet rocks and clackers were? Quadruple digits? Anyhow, they became best sellers. Hula Hoops, Cabbage Patch Dolls, Ninja Turtles, Power Rangers, and Pokemon are all products whose price exceeded value because they became hot. They became contagious. All of them all but died out as well because if something's not built on real value, it dies out when the next hot commodity hits the marketplace.

Distinction that is based on real value has staying power. This occurs when price exceeds a logical and normal price, but people are still willing to pay it. Coca-Cola, BMW, FedEx, and IBM all are brands of distinction. They can charge more because of who they are. People recognize their names and logos, and that is worth something to them. My kids all want to wear expensive Abercrombie & Fitch clothing, even though better-made clothing can be bought cheaper elsewhere. I myself often reach for the name-brand products at the grocery store instead of the cheaper generic brand. What's inside is probably all the same, but I recognize a name.

This is what branding is all about and why it's crucial to businesses today. Businesses that do not have recognizable brands often fail to businesses that do. The catch is that establishing distinction can often be scary and requires boldness to pull it off successfully. This is the crossroad I referred to earlier. When the lines of value and price start coming together, it is much easier to simply try to widen the gap by lowering price or adding something of little value. It's quick and easy and doesn't require much strategy. Creating a brand, on the other hand, is not so simple and takes a little time.

The best example of the crossroad occurred about seven years ago with K-Mart and Target. Both were in a desperate battle with Wal-Mart. One decided to try the quick fix of lowering price by bringing back the "blue light." The other, Target, decided it could not beat Wal-Mart at its own game and sought to build its own brand. While K-Mart had some quick, early successes, they were not positioned to withstand the test of time. Target was slower in its initial growth, but was building something to last. As of my writing, Target is flourishing, and K-Mart is retooling once again. Target took a bleak situation and made something out of it by creating distinction. It wasn't the easier road, but it was a better road, a more contagious road. They started to click with the public once they defined who they were and how they were different. Wal-Mart had given them lemons, and they made lemonade.

Paul Revere, Milton Bradley, and Target are not alone. We live in a world of contagious businesses and contagious people who know how to click and are dedicated to doing so. They are in banks, gas stations, pizza joints, and libraries. They're in sports, run businesses, star in movies, hold public office, join the military, and drive shuttle vans. The only question is: Are you among them? Better yet, will you be among them in the future? I was eating lunch the other day and flipped open my *USA Today* and came across an ad for Infiniti automobiles. It caught my attention because it read: "rare, spontaneous, unexpected, bold, curious, intriguing, intuitive, fearless, unusual, audacious, brash, undaunted, irreverent, daring, dynamic, maverick, unbridled, soulful, provocative, strong, wild, unwavering, romantic, genuine, unorthodox, brave, renegade, radical, visionary, dreamer." If I didn't know better, I'd think it was an ad for contagious people.

In fact, I'll even mention some of those qualities in the forthcoming chapters. I'll introduce 10 "contagions" that contribute in some way to clicking with others. Some in big ways, others in more subtle ways. With each contagion, we'll look at both the inward and outward qualities that make up each one. Each one has inward qualities that help you become someone others want to click with, and outward qualities to help you click with them. With some contagions, I'll begin with the inward qualities, with others the outer, depending on how each one can be best learned.

Clicking is a two-way street, not just between you and another person, but between the inner and outer you as well. In other words, it's one thing to "act" contagious, but for real clicking to take place, you must also BE contagious. You must BE first, the DOING will naturally follow. The outward qualities help you demonstrate outwardly what's going on inside. Plus, they help you build the habits needed for contagious clicking. I believe if you do something long enough, you'll become it. Bottom line: The outward helps the inward, and the inward helps the outward.

So let's get into it. Let's look at the 10 "contagions," inside and out, that will help you click with everyone every time!

3

Contagious Principle #1: Confidence

Though the contagious principles that I discuss in this book are of no particular order, the contagion of confidence is without a doubt the most visible and somewhat most obvious. It's also ironically the most fragile quality. Confidence shines through your every movement. It comes through the eyes, is heard through the voice, seen in the bounce of your step, how you walk, your handshake, and even how you sit.

Add all this up and you have presence. Presence is defined in the Webster's dictionary as a person of great personage. I'm not sure that tells you much, but I do like that word, personage. It's the total you, the total package. Confidence in each area of your personage gives you a contagious presence. Former President Bill Clinton, love him or hate him, has great presence. He's more than six feet tall, smiles readily, and has good eye contact. He might lack other contagions, but confidence he has in great abundance. I believe that is one of the primary reasons for his political success. We want our leaders to have confidence, and every good leader does.

It is impossible to be an effective leader and lack confidence for two reasons. First, if they don't believe they'll be an effective leader in their hearts, it is impossible to pretend for too long a period of time. Second, if they truly aren't confident in themselves, they'll lose the respect of those they are leading. It's interesting that one reason was inward and one was outward.

In fact, each and every contagion that I'll talk about in this book has inward qualities and outward qualities. Each contagion manifests itself in ways seen and unseen. Both are necessary to be able to genuinely, and naturally, click with others. It's nice to do the things that make you contagious; it's another to BE contagious.

For example, one can play the part of being confident for a while, but ultimately the act will be exposed. I've known people who went through assertiveness training classes to learn to be more confident. All they learned was how to act more confidently in some situations. They addressed the symptoms without changing who they were. They were unconfident people acting confidently. The problem with this is obvious. Once this is recognized, the person loses all credibility and power to lead. So, you're probably asking, "Can an unconfident person ever learn to be confident?" It's the 10-million-dollar question of this book. The answer is a resounding yes. But that change must happen from the inside out. It can't happen merely by doing. It must happen by believing. It must be authentic.

What about the experts who preach that you can change inwardly by doing outwardly? Is this true? The answer is yes, but only temporarily. This is the problem with most self-help books in my opinion. They give you the what to do's that work in the short term, but leave you bewildered when the euphoria of the moment wears off. Outward is important, but only as a manifestation of the inward. We act confident because we are confident.

Confidence, like all the contagions, is a magnetic quality that draws people and circumstances to you like a magnet. They work. They work because you have the contagion inwardly and you show it outwardly. I guess you could get some benefit by just doing some of the outwardly things we discuss. You could, theoretically, click with

" Confidence is competence "

some people by doing the things that lead to clicking, but that's not the kind of clicking that is contagious. That's a hollow clicking. We want to click because we are "click-able." That starts on the inside.

TALENTS, GIFTS, AND ABILITIES

The inward journey of developing true confidence starts with taking inventory of your talents, skills, and abilities. These might seem to be synonymous, but they are very different. Talents are inward things. They are God-given gifts. They are sometimes easy to recognize and other times are not so obvious. My friend Charles was given the unique gift of empathy. He can sit for hours and do nothing but listen, nod his head, and comfort another person. I've painfully watched him do it countless times. If it were me, I'd say, "Get over it," and "good luck." Patience is not one of my gifts. I, on the other hand, have the gift of gab. I am one of those rare, (some might say weird) creatures who could get up at 2:00 in the morning out of a deep sleep and speak to 10,000 people without blinking an eye. My mother proclaimed when I was a little boy that I'd be one of two things when I grew up: a salesperson or a preacher. It was prophetic, because I kind of do both. I make my living preaching about sales and customer service.

You might not have this talent (you're probably thankful for that), but you definitely have one. Recognizing your gifts is essential for building and cultivating confidence. When you're confident, you believe in yourself. When you believe in yourself, you exude presence. When you exude presence, you are contagious. When you are contagious, you click. It doesn't end there. When you consistently click, you attract success. Finding true confidence begins with recognizing your talent. You've heard of ROI (Return on Investment), well, I believe in ROA, Return on Ability. The greatest and fastest on return on effort is through your natural ability. Everyone has a natural ability, and finding yours begins with asking yourself this question, "What do I love to do when time and money are of no concern?" There's no right or wrong answer. There's also no answer that's too small. Your love and desire for something is the prime indicator of your gifts and abilities.

I once knew a guy who was employed as a printer, but his true love was baseball cards. He got hooked when he was a kid and was still hooked as an adult. He just couldn't shake his desire for collecting baseball cards. It was all he could think about. He even considered therapy at the advice of a girlfriend who diagnosed his passion as "not wanting to grow up." Well, she might have hit on a bit of truth, but what's wrong with that? Who says that once we reach a certain age, we need to lose all childhood passions?

We'll talk more about passion in another chapter. For now, I'll stick to finding your gifts and building confidence. Back to my story, today this young man makes a nice living buying and selling vintage baseball collectibles. He's happy, contented, inwardly and outwardly confident, and he loves what he does. I'd say he's successful.

My sister went to high school with John Mayer. You probably know who he is if you have teenagers in the house. He's a newly popular young rock musician. I have to admit, I like his music. My sister tells me that for the brief time she knew John Mayer, he and his guitar were practically inseparable. He rarely went anywhere without it, and he became known simply as "the guy with the guitar." He began playing because he thought it was a good way to meet girls. While he might have thought that, the seeds of gifts are planted well before one realizes it. Nonetheless, he became so sure of his gifts and abilities, he used to practice his autograph in anticipation of one day someone requesting it. His confidence continued to grow, and hard work has paid off. His gift has always been his music, but now, the whole world knows it.

Steven Spielberg was given the talent to produce movies. As a young boy, he made home movies with Barbie Dolls as actors. Making movies was his passion, and from that his confidence flourished.

Gifts can also be very subtle things. I have a friend who at age 44 believes he still has not found his gifts. I beg to differ. He is one of the most logical thinkers I know. While I sometimes get swept away in the riptide of emotion, he has the ability to fast forward in his mind to predict outcomes. Is it any wonder he's in the insurance business? He sees this as a curse, but it's definitely a gift. Another person I know is the absolute best hugger I've ever met. Someone else I know has the uncanny knack of finding a bargain. Another friend amazes me with her perception. She can spot a rabbit hopping through the grass from 200 feet away, or smell a rose from across a room. While these might not be the kind of gifts that lead to fame and fortune, they are still indeed gifts.

So take inventory right now of your gifts. Recognize your gifts by your passions and interests. Write them down. If you only come up with one or two, that's OK. That's the way it is for most of us. If you have trouble even coming up with one, go ask a friend. Sometimes it takes someone outside ourselves to see things we're not able to see!

Skills are a bit different. Skills are things we've learned. Skills might or might not have anything to do with our God-given talents. I've been given the gift of speech and hence have come to develop the skills to enhance my gift. My friend Marty, on the other hand, has the gift of drawing, but his career requires him to develop other kinds of skills. We'll talk about the learned skills of confidence a little later in this chapter, but for now, write down all the tangible skills you've learned through the years. Nothing is too small. Remember things like learning how a smile can defuse a tense moment, or learning when to keep your mouth shut. These might not be skills you list on a resume, but they are still skills. Stop now and begin your list. It might take a while, but that's OK. I'll be here when you get back. When you're done, see if there are any skills listed that align with your gifts. It's sometimes interesting (not to mention confidence building) to see that, more often than not, we've developed skills that are in harmony with our talents.

Abilities are different yet again. They are things you are capable of doing, but haven't, either because you haven't learned the skills or you haven't identified your talent. They are the unrealized extension of gifts and skills. I won't suggest having you write another list, but know that listing what you're capable of would be an endless task.

The point behind taking inventory of talents, skills, and abilities is to come to the realization that you are uniquely special and in that, we can find confidence. No one else on the planet has the identical list of talents, skills, and abilities as you. Real confidence always flows inside out. It has to be inside before we can show it outside. Recognizing and finding peace with WHO you are is the first step in developing real confidence. The total package of talents, skills, and abilities is your personage. It's unique, special, and for better or worse, it's you. We must feel good about ourselves before anyone else will. This isn't to say we don't have things about ourselves we like more than others. I don't like my impatience. It does mean however, that our weaknesses will never diminish our strengths. Our confidence should remain strong in spite of a few imperfections. I believe the purpose of our imperfections is to keep us humble.

HUMILITY

Humility is every bit as important to real confidence as self-esteem. Humility grounds us and protects us from developing false confidence. Some might refer to "false confidence" as overconfidence, but that's not really accurate. It's not that someone gets overly confident; it's more like they get falsely confident. False confidence occurs when someone loses sight of his or her imperfections. Imperfections connect you with others, not alienate you from others. Whenever you give the false impression that you have no flaws, others will find them for you.

When I first started my speaking career, I wrongly believed that audiences would find me more credible if I were perfect. I strived to create the perfect speech and carried myself as if I were the most important person in the room. What a mistake! No one is perfect, and when we try to give that impression, it backfires. Our confidence is made perfect in our weaknesses. It took me a while, but I finally caught on. Audiences didn't expect, nor want me to be perfect. Speaking (much like clicking) is not about you or me; it's about the other person. It wasn't until I abandoned my pursuit of perfection that I started clicking with audiences.

In his book titled, *The 100 Simple Secrets of Happy People*, author David Niven states this delicate balance of confidence and false confidence wonderfully. He writes, "Believe in yourself, but don't believe in yourself too much." On the surface this looks like double speak, but I believe he's saying that it's great to believe in ourselves, but don't let your confidence turn into arrogance. It's a delicate balance. You want to be confident, but not arrogant. Humility keeps this happening and is what allows us to click. Many people are confident, and many are humble, but very few are both. Part of the problem is that somewhere along the way, we've come to equate humility with weakness.

The truth is it's the exact other way around. We become stronger by acknowledging our weaknesses. By not acknowledging them, they become a greater force in our lives. Secure is the person that recognizes their weaknesses; insecure is the person who won't (or can't) admit them. An interesting thing happens when we allow our humility to show. We click. People are drawn to people who are secure enough in themselves to be vulnerable. Real confidence is contagious, and the primary way to display your confidence is through humility.

So let's review. Recognize and celebrate your talents, skills, and abilities, mix in a dose of humility, and you will be a shining, contagious example of real confidence. Now you're ready to supplement your confidence with outward actions.

The journey of developing outward confidence is more specific and scientific, but as I've stated before, it depends solely on the inner. You might learn a few tricks of the confidence trade, but they'll ultimately be exposed if they aren't congruent with how you see yourself inside. This relationship between outward performance and inward self-image is an important dynamic of congruency and one that I'll devote an entire chapter to later in this book. For now, let's stick with a few outward skills to cultivate your confidence.

BODY LANGUAGE

First, let's look at body language. People make snap judgments about you based solely on your body language. I've known clients who've admitted to me that they've made decisions about doing business with someone in the first few seconds of meeting them. I've read that this window of first impressions can be anywhere from three seconds to one minute, but in either case, it's really quick. Our minds are capable of processing hundreds of pieces of information at a time, and this is most evident during a first encounter with someone. This is known as sizing you up. They are evaluating your personage. (You can tell I like that word.) While no one part of you is any more important to clicking than another, human nature tells us that we are naturally drawn to people's faces. That's why a smile, or lack thereof, is the first thing people notice. A smile is the universal gesture. It doesn't matter what country you're in, people know a smile as a gesture of friendliness. But not all smiles are created equal. Just as confidence must be tempered with humility to be effective for clicking, a smile must be tempered with sincerity to establish a connection. It's not easy to articulate the difference between a sincere and insincere smile, but it's easy to recognize. Sincere smiles radiate from within, while insincere ones are nothing more than facial maneuvering. You can make a smiley face, but that's not a real smile. We might make a smiley face to a stranger in a grocery store, but that smile is very different from the ones we give our best friends after not seeing them for a while. The difference is emotion. A smiley face is emotionless; a "click-able" smile is warm and inviting. This kind of smile exudes confidence and invites the other person to interact with you without hesitation.

Just as crucial to rapport is the body language that accompanies your smile, and no single gesture is as important as a handshake, especially in business settings. I'm continually amazed in my presentations at the number of people who underestimate the role of a handshake. Men think it's a show of machismo, while women often don't think about it at all. Handshaking is a form of communication that sets the tone of the relationship. I love to ask men if they should shake a woman's hand differently than they shake a man's? The answers I get usually vary by generation. Older men say they should always wait for the woman to offer her hand first, and the handshake should be softer and gentler than with a man. What's interesting is that the women in the room, regardless of age, usually shake their heads in disapproval to this answer. I follow up with a question to the women asking them if they've ever decided not to do business with a man based solely on his handshake? Invariably, many hands shoot up. An equal number of guys look dazed and confused. They had no idea that decisions were being made based on the way they shook hands. Such is the case for clicking. We might eventually recognize when we click, but we often have no clue when we don't. Rarely will someone tell us when there just isn't a connection, and to that point, no one dares confess that a handshake doomed the relationship. A handshake should be gender neutral. For the guys, a handshake should not be a show of strength. Your grip should be firm and direct, but it shouldn't hurt. It should be a friendly gesture, not an intimidating one. It impresses no one if you hurt his or her hand with your brute strength. The basic rules are as follows:

- Always keep your right hand free. The left hand should hold only one item.

- Extend your hand with fingers extended and thumb up.

- Shake from the elbow, not from wrist or shoulder.

- Make direct eye contact.

In social situations (and when overseas), you should wait for the woman to offer her hand first, but never in American business situations.[1] Women want, and should, be treated as peers, and some of the gentlemanly rules of etiquette past are not always appreciated in business settings. I'll go even one step further. In business, the person who extends their hand first tends to get the upper hand in the interaction. "Why?" you might ask. The answer lies in confidence. People with greater and deeper levels of confidence generally are quick to smile, shake hands, and introduce themselves, while those who lack confidence also lack initiative. It's one big happy cycle. When you smile and shake hands readily and properly, you exude confidence, and when you exude confidence, you click, and when you click, you feed your confidence.

Confidence is a contagion that must be seen and felt. Confidence that is seen but not felt is often perceived as arrogance. Confidence that is felt but not seen lacks clicking power. Confidence, like all the contagions, has inward and outward qualities. One without the other is diluted. Start by cultivating your inner confidence. Mix in a dash of outer know-how, and your confidence will begin to bloom. Someone with blooming, yet humble confidence is highly contagious!

Quick Click Tip

Complete your inventory of talents, gifts, and abilities, and read it every day before bed and first thing in the morning. If you do this long enough and consistently, you will start to believe it, and you can only begin to act confidently once you believe in yourself. Then it's simply a matter of projecting outwardly what you know and feel inwardly, but staying humble. There's a fine line between confidence and arrogance. One clicks, the other clashes!

---

[1] Rules of nonverbal communication vary greatly outside the United States. It would be wise to do a bit of homework as to the cultural differences before traveling abroad or doing business with people who might be from another country.

4

Contagious Principle #2: Curiosity

Now that you're on your way to developing clicking confidence, the next step is to focus that energy toward the other person. If too much focus and attention is on you, then you alienate yourself and handicap rapport. But, like confidence and humility, it's a delicate balance. Too much or forced attention on other people will make them uncomfortable and suspicious. Too little attention on people, and they will lose interest quickly and the opportunity to click might be lost. The best way to focus your attention on another person without being obvious or overbearing is to develop the contagion of curiosity.

For curiosity to be contagious, it needs to go deeper than just being curious. We need to develop a sincere interest in learning about other people; and just as with confidence, there are both inward and outward qualities of clicking curiosity.

The inward aspect has two parts to it: wonder and vulnerability. Developing a sense of wonder is a magical quality that not only is contagious to others, but does wonders for us as well. Vulnerability is the quality that invites people to get to know us. In any sincere clicking connection, both parties need to be at least partially vulnerable to the other. Let's begin with wonder.

WONDER

Developing a sense of wonder begins with training yourself to look beyond what you see with your eyes. Being able to see the beauty behind the object always has and always will be a highly contagious quality. It's hard to explain, but its roots are in people's deep-seated desire to be inspired. Especially in today's world, people crave inspiration, and if you are someone who is naturally full of wonder, it can and will inspire others. Have you ever slowed down enough to sit on a park bench and watch people? Have you ever watched a spider build its web? How about a bird taking a bath? Have you ever wondered what a dog was thinking? Have you ever watched a thunderstorm in the distance while flying at 30,000 feet? Have you ever looked deep into a person's eyes?

I was always fascinated with the stars. At five years old, I knew which planet was called the Blue Planet, and which had polar ice caps. I had my own telescope at six, and spent countless hours staring at the night sky. I remember getting so frustrated at the idea that space never ends. It's still a subject that is beyond my ability to comprehend. Each and every August, late at night, one can witness spectacular meteor showers. When I was a boy, this event would be the lead story on the news. Today, it's regulated to a passing remark before a commercial break if it's even mentioned at all. Brennan Manning, author of *The Ragamuffin Gospel*, writes, "By and large, our world has lost its sense of wonder. We have grown up. We no longer catch our breath at the sight of a rainbow or the scent of a rose, as we once did. We have grown bigger and everything else smaller, less impressive."

The power of a sense of wonder hit home with me one hot summer night when I was a teenager. I was sitting on the edge of a field with a girl I had a huge crush on. We were looking at the stars and I was doing my best to be romantic when suddenly she looked at me with a slight tear in her eye, and said, "This is the most magical night of my life." At that moment I realized that my sense of wonder and appreciation for the stars had rubbed off on her, and for at least that moment, created a special connection. We clicked. I'm sure we both remember that night to this day, even though we never became boyfriend and girlfriend. The lesson, however, was clear.

Wonder creates magical moments that, in turn, create rapport. Wonder forces attention off ourselves and puts it on the world around us. Without wonder, human tendency is to become too self-preoccupied. Wonder lets you see the world that many miss. It lets others know there's more to us than meets the eye. Wonder is what Robert Kennedy had in mind when he said, "Some men see things as they are and say why. I dream things that never were and say why not." To get a greater sense of wonder, expand and use your imagination.

A wonderful way to do this is to spend an afternoon with a six-year-old. If you don't have one, borrow one. Of course, I'd highly suggest you get the parents' permission first. Our imaginations are at its peak at age six. Kids see wonder and excitement in everything. Kids see a tree, and their first thought is how high they can climb it. We adults see a tree, and we think of having to rake its leaves. Kids see a rain puddle and race to jump over it. We adults, fearing we might get a little wet, think that's a dumb idea and wouldn't dare to resort to such childish behavior. Kids see a stick and they see a potential toy. We see a stick. Put it down before your hands get dirty. What's happened to us?

Our sense of wonder has declined right along with our imaginations, but it's like any other skill or ability. If we don't use it, we'll lose it. We need to be full of wonder before we can see wonder. I believe we must build it back up by getting excited again at the little things in life. Let's not wait until something exciting happens to get excited; let's get excited first. In the old science lesson about cause and effect, it's important to note that wonder and excitement are a cause, not an effect. If we condition ourselves to see wonder and be excited, then wonderful and exciting things will happen—not only in the area of clicking with others, but in all parts of our life as well.

Wonder makes us appreciative. It keeps us humble and helps us to always look for the beauty in things. These qualities are highly contagious. Wonder is a contagion that can attract others to your doorstep. Vulnerability, on the other hand, invites them in.

VULNERABILITY

Like humility, somewhere along the way, we've come to falsely believe that vulnerability is a sign of weakness. That can't be further from the truth. People who are truly weak go to great lengths to appear strong and invincible. They build themselves up by appearing to be perfect. This is a hollow existence.

Now don't get me wrong. I'm not suggesting that you spill out your life problems to everyone you meet. Being vulnerable isn't about wearing your trials and tribulations on your sleeve; it's about being open and receptive. A good example is people who get hurt by relationships and consequently build walls around their feelings and don't let others know their true feelings in fear of getting hurt again.

The opposite of being vulnerable is being hardened. Hardening often has the reverse effect. It might cause more hurt by driving others away than it would if the person were open and receptive. Being open doesn't mean letting every emotion come pouring out. As with all contagions, there's a fine line to being vulnerable and being a victim. You don't want to elicit sympathy. That's the role of the victim. Being open and receptive simply means that you won't let past failures and heartaches harden you. I've talked to many people who have become so hardened by their pasts that they sometimes don't even recognize themselves anymore. They miss opportunities because they were too guarded and hardened. I'm reminded of the old baseball cliché that you can't steal second base with one foot on first base. You have to take a chance.

Life is like that. You must be willing to get hurt. It doesn't feel good, but the alternative hurts even more. Hardened people don't click. Open, receptive, and optimistic people do.

The outward qualities of curiosity are basic tenets to communication: asking questions and listening. There are no greater persuasive skills than asking questions and listening, but there's so much more to them than you might think. If clicking is your goal, asking questions doesn't only involve your mouth, but your heart as well. You must be sincerely interested in the other person. Listening involves more than your ears, but your mind and full focus and attention. The rest of this chapter will be devoted to understanding and being a clicking kind of communicator.

ASKING QUESTIONS

When I was little, my mother would respond to my incessant questions by saying, "What is this, 20 questions?" She didn't mean any harm, but I was just curious. We learn by asking questions. I cringe when I hear of teachers who stifle questions or worse yet, ridicule a student for asking a stupid question. Nothing worthwhile was ever accomplished without someone asking questions.

One could even argue that asking a question is the starting point of any achievement. Sir Isaac Newton might have asked why the apple fell down instead of up. Columbus might have been curious about what would happen if he sailed west. Benjamin Franklin might have asked why he felt a shock while flying a kite in a thunderstorm. You get the drift. On a less dramatic level, businesses need to ask questions to determine who to hire, sales people need to ask for the business, someone needs to ask another's hand in marriage, and politicians' need to ask for your vote. Everything begins with asking questions, and clicking is no exception.

There are, of course, right and wrong ways to ask questions if your goal is to click with someone. The wrong ways include disinterested asking and ulterior asking.

Disinterested question asking is self-explanatory. It is asking questions when you really don't care about the answers. It's like you're just going through the motions. Your mind is somewhere else, not fully interested in the answers. It's like a passerby saying, "How are you?" In most cases, the asker has passed us by before we can even utter a reply. In this case, the question was more a courtesy than a question. The asker wasn't at all interested in the answer.

Ulterior question asking is where there is an ulterior motive for asking. This is where the asker is obviously very interested in the answers, but for selfish gain, not simply just to build rapport. This kind of question-asking is usually characterized by a shotgun method of asking, rapid fire, one question right after another. Sales people often fall into this trap. They know they must ask questions, and so does the customer, so they resort to getting through them as fast as possible. This is one of the many reasons why loyalty in business is at an all-time low. For the most part, sales people do not know how to ask questions to build rapport instead of just information gathering.

Asking questions to click has several parts to it: Why you ask, what to ask, how you ask, and when to ask. The why should be answered by the mere fact that you're reading this book. You should ask questions because you are curious and genuinely interested in getting to know another person. I assume that if you weren't genuinely interested in clicking, you'd be reading something else right now. So we'll leave the why as is.

What to ask is easy. You should be asking questions about them. Asking questions about them is the perfect opportunity to practice your curiosity. Be curious about what they've said. One question should naturally lead to the next. If they've told you they worked in a restaurant, ask which restaurant, what they do for their restaurant, how they got started, do they like it, do they want to work there long-term or is it just a short-term assignment, etc. The questions you ask display your curiosity, and the degree in which you appear sincerely interested will be the exact degree in which you aid in clicking.

Another element in clicking is also present in your question asking, and that is spontaneity. How fast can you think on your feet? The dynamic is genuine curiosity. The premise is that if you truly are curious and interested, you'll know exactly what question to ask next. Your curiosity will lead you. If you're only going through the motions, you will be less spontaneous and your questions won't flow easily. Spontaneity is hard to fake. What to ask begins with the why you ask, which begins with being naturally curious, which begins with a sense of wonder. It's a great big endless cycle. Contagions must work in harmony if you want to genuinely click. One contagion alone is not sufficient. That's why before we talk about outward skills, we first talk about inward qualities. What to ask and why you ask are linked by inward qualities.

How to ask questions is a science in itself and one I'll tackle in greater detail in the very next chapter, but suffice it to say, it is a crucial element in clicking.

When to ask questions, and when to stop asking questions is a lot trickier. You certainly won't click by launching into 20 questions after your handshake. There should always be a pause between your initial greeting and commencement of a dialogue, and permission to proceed procured with nonverbal communication. This would include a brief meeting of the eyes, a physical lingering in your presence, or if the person asks you a question first. Any of these nonverbal cues gives you permission to be curious. This, of course, is not a foolproof equation, but it's a good rule of thumb.

Conversely, there is a point in which your curiosity begins to be annoying and it's time to stop asking questions. That point varies and requires some perception on your part. If the other person's answers to your questions get shorter with each question, it's time to end the questions. Similarly, if they begin to look away or past you as you're talking, you've lost their attention and it's best not to press on so as not to permanently damage rapport. Just as in poker, there's a time to hold 'em and there's a time to fold 'em; with clicking, there's a time to ask questions and there's a time to just plain shut up.

LISTENING

Which leads us to the communications complement to asking questions: listening. You can display your curiosity every bit as much through listening as you can through asking. Listening requires active participation. It's not a time to sit back and doodle. Listening is hard work, and people are starving to be listened to. Our society has become so hurried that real, undistracted listening has almost become extinct. That's why it's such an important element in clicking with others. People want it, yet rarely get it.

There's also a great myth in communications in that many people believe talking is power. In the world of rapport, the exact opposite is true. It's the person who is listening that is in control of the interaction. To optimize your odds of clicking, you should talk 25 percent of the time or less, and listen 75 percent or greater. You might ask the right questions at the right time, and in the right way, but if you aren't a good listener, all is lost. So what constitutes a *good* listener? I believe being a good listener (that is one that clicks) has two parts to it. First, we must work on being a good listener, and second, we must allow the other person to know we are indeed listening. In other words, it isn't effective for clicking to be a great listener unless the other person *believes* we are listening. There's an inward (surprise) and outward element to listening. Inward includes our listening skills; outward is the physical appearance of listening. Let's explore how to listen first.

Ironically, there's no utopia in listening in that no one is ever a perfect listener. Listening is always a work in progress. You might be a perfect listener in one interaction, and the world's worst in another. There's been many a book written on listening alone, so my remarks will only begin to skim the top of the water. Listening is far more complex than most people realize. Listening is not hearing. Hearing is done with the ears; listening is done with the mind. To be an effective listener, you must focus your entire being on the other person. This is much easier said than done because our minds are capable of processing information much faster than the person can deliver it. The slower the rate of speech by the other person, the more susceptible our minds are to wandering. Slowing your mind down to the rate of speech requires great concentration and practice. There's no magic to the formula, just good old-fashioned focus power to avoid the five common distractions. They are:

1. **Thinking Ahead.** You might be nodding your head in compliance, but your mind is 20 paces ahead. You might be so far ahead that you're preparing a mental grocery list for your evening shopping trip. This also includes thinking of what to say next or how to respond. Either way, you're ahead of the other person.

2. **Thinking Behind.** This is the polar opposite of the above-mentioned. You're stuck 20 paces behind. Maybe because you're trying to interpret or evaluate a previous statement or just thinking about a past event. Either way, you're behind.

3. **Mental Warfare.** This is where you are debating in your mind the validity of something they've said. You're mentally combing through the annals of your brain to affirm or discredit their words. Either way, you're not with them.

4. **Physical Distraction.** This is where you become distracted by something physical about them. It could be a scar, or ponytail, or a weird tie. It also includes being attracted to them. It's hard to be a good listener when you're thinking about how attractive they might be. The same is true for finding them unattractive. Either way, you are distracted.

5. **Impatience**. This is where you are either too busy or too disinterested to remain focused enough to listen effectively. Either way, there's no way you'll click.

Even the very best listeners are guilty of at least one of these distractions during every interaction; the trick is to catch yourself and refocus. Hopefully the other person has not noticed your distraction.

The outward appearance of listening is no less important. For listening to become an aid in clicking, the other person MUST believe you are truly listening. As far as clicking is concerned, you're better off to not be listening but have them think you are than the other way around. Having another person think you're listening involves eye contact, follow up questions, and listening gestures.

Eye contact is a must. Nothing signals nonlistening faster than to be talking to someone who is looking elsewhere. I know of no better example of focused eye contact than my friend and colleague, Glenna Salsbury. I'll mention her again in a later chapter. When you talk to her, it's as if nothing else is going on in the world. She has mastered the ability to completely shut out her surroundings and give undivided attention to the other person. I've watched as people literally shouted her name from across the room, and her eye contact never wavered. This is truly a clicking advantage and one she takes full advantage of.

Follow-up questions let the other person know that you've been following along, but don't fake it. Asking the wrong or inappropriate follow-up question can be damaging to clicking. Do not confuse follow-up questions with a restatement of something they've just said. Some people believe it's a good listening technique to restate or paraphrase something another person has said. While this might be helpful if you need to clarify something that was said, I do not think it's good for clicking. Rapport is best created by asking a follow-up question rather than merely restating their words.

Then, finally, listening gestures complete the puzzle. An occasional nod, smile, or change in facial expression is both affirming and persuasive. But be careful. Overuse of the same gesture can have the reverse effect. Someone who nods incessantly gives the impression that they are trying to disguise their disinterest. Further proof, too much of a contagion dose is just as detrimental as too little. The best thing to do is to be present and let your gestures flow naturally. Nod, smile, or frown as the dialogue dictates, not because you think it's time.

Curiosity can be a highly contagious quality, but remember that curiosity can kill the cat as well. Curiosity, like all the contagions, is not something you do; it's something you are. It's innocent, sincere, childlike, and completely void of ulterior motives. Developing this kind of curiosity will connect you with others in ways you've never dreamed possible.

Quick Click Tip

Curiosity is a doubled-edge contagion. It draws others closer to you and draws you closer to others. Make it a point to find out three new things about someone you either know or meet every day, and one new thing about the world around you. You might need to remind yourself to do this at first, but eventually it will become second nature. If you become more interested in others, others will become more interested in you!

5

Contagious Principle #3: Connectedness

Speaking of connecting, the contagion of connectedness is more science than art. There's an entire arsenal of connecting tools that is essential if you want to click with everyone every time. Mistakenly, connecting is often seen as synonymous with clicking, but I see connectedness as an ingredient of clicking. Unlike other contagions that begin inwardly and manifest themselves outwardly, connectedness is almost entirely outward. It is the most deliberate of all contagions. I often refer to this contagion in my seminars as "rapport technology," because mastering connectedness is, in my opinion, as much a technology as computers and rocket science.

Connectedness occurs through our senses: sight, touch, and sound. Taste and smell can also be a tool in connecting, but they connect us more with inanimate objects and places rather than people. For instance, a certain smell might automatically and subconsciously connect us with our grandmother's kitchen. Sight, touch, and sound will do that as well, but I'll limit my remarks to what they do in connecting us with other people.

Like any one of my contagions, there are countless books on connecting. I personally know of several speakers who make their living speaking on this topic. It's a complex subject and has many facets to it. Whether or not you connect with someone is highly subjective, and what works one time might not work the next. It's very personal. Our methods, to be an effective tool for clicking, must vary as we deal with different types of people. You should follow their lead.

Following their lead simply means to be alert and sensitive as to how they are communicating with you and let their methods dictate the interaction. This calls for a major overhaul of the Golden Rule that our moms and dads taught us as children. They taught us to treat others the way WE would want to be treated. That's great in theory, but practically speaking, it's quite selfish and potentially damaging to clicking. Another person might not want to be treated the same way we would. By treating others according to what feels good to us, we limit the potential to click with more people. We click with people who enjoy and prefer our methods of communicating, but we don't click with the rest. If unselfish clicking is what you're after, then you must alter your perception and application of the Golden Rule. The "Clicking" Golden Rule is: *Treat others the way THEY want to be treated.*

Friend and colleague Tony Alessandra calls this "The Platinum Rule" and has written an excellent book of the same title. In it he explores the four basic personality types and how to relate to each one. I'm not sure I subscribe to the notion that everyone falls neatly into one of four personality types, but I strongly agree with adapting our communication to match theirs. We should follow their lead and communicate with them the way they are choosing to communicate with us. By doing this, we can click by choice, and not by chance.

Now some might be thinking that following their lead is manipulative and not natural, but that's not so. We communicate differently all the time. It depends on how we feel, where we are, whom we're with, and what we're doing. The Clicking Golden Rule suggests that you communicate not based on you, but on them. This doesn't mean we're being fake. I'm not suggesting that you be something you're not. I'm merely suggesting that you be alert and sensitive to how others communicate and to follow their lead. By learning how to connect by following their lead instead of forcing your own, you'll have the potential to click with everyone every time.

SIGHT

Let's begin with the first of our senses that can be used to connect with others, and that is sight, what we see. This includes physical appearances and our eyes themselves. We live in a visual world and without fail, faces, (especially the eyes), are the first thing we notice about others and others notice about us. Let's talk about facial expression first. So much can be said or not said through facial expression without uttering a single word.

Here is just an extremely partial listing of the array of emotions that can be conveyed through facial expression: happiness, sadness, intimidation, frustration, tiredness, pain, boredom, excitement, anticipation, skepticism, amazement, restraint, and concentration, just to mention a few. Because faces are the first thing people notice, they are often the primary factor in first impressions, and first impressions are crucial to clicking.

I'm sure I don't have to impress upon you the importance of first impressions. You know they're important, but have you ever wondered why? Why are first impressions so hard to overcome? The answer lies in the way our brains think. I don't want to get too scientific here, but our brains are very organized machines. We remember things that happen first and things that happen last. The in-between is more easily forgotten and stored in a different part of the brain.

We always remember our firsts. We remember our first day of school, our first date, our first kiss, our first car, and our first job. First impressions are right in there as well. Most married people can recall in vivid detail the first time they met their spouse. If you ask them to recall their second or third encounter, our memories are a lot fuzzier.

Our brains seem hard-wired to remember firsts. [1] For this reason, first impressions count for more than subsequent impressions. You rarely get a second chance to click. Facial expression is tied to first impression and first impression to rapport. It's a fairly simple equation.

So what does your face say when you meet someone new? Are you happy to meet new people, or are you nervous at the thought? Do you smile readily (more on that in a later chapter) or do you force a makeshift smile? Are you confident (hey, that sounds familiar) and self-assured, or are you tentative and awkward? The answer is in your face.

More specifically, it's in your eyes. The eyes are called the window to our soul, and for good reason. The eyes signal "approachability." Approachability is how approachable you are perceived to be by others. People who click have levels of approachability, while those who are socially timid and awkward have lower levels. The eyes tell someone if you are comfortable and receptive to clicking. They communicate your desire to get to know them. It's kind of like flirting, but with no other motive in mind except connecting in that single moment in time. Traditional flirting might have a future objective. "Clicking" flirting's only objective is to connect in the moment only. Other than that, connecting and flirting involve the same dynamics. Both are tools to build a relationship. Both are heavily dependent on the eyes.

It's through the eyes that many contagions are displayed. Try this exercise sometime. Find someone that you either know well or want to get to know better. Then sit and stare into their eyes for a solid five minutes. I guarantee that after five minutes of silent eye contact, you will feel more connected to that person than if you had spent an hour talking. Eyes have a way of bonding people quicker than anything else. Caution: This exercise can be very intimate. I cannot be held responsible for the actions that might follow!

---

[1] Interestingly, in an informal survey conducted by my office, 77 percent of people remember their first-grade teacher while only 39 percent can recall their second-grade teacher.

If you're in sales, I believe the eyes are your greatest selling tools. People read your eyes and come to split-second impressions based on what they see. They want to see confidence, conviction, cheerfulness, curiosity, connectability, and the rest of the 10 contagions. Contrary to what you might think, communication is mostly nonverbal, with your eyes and facial expression leading the way. The oft-quoted Dr. Albert Mehrabian's classic book, *Silent Messages*, explores this in greater detail. His research concluded that in spoken communication, words represent only 7 percent of the total message, 93 percent is in the way we say the words, and in facial expression. What others *see* speaks louder than what you say. Too often, we spend far too much time perfecting the message at the expense of the messenger and more often than not, that messenger is your eyes. To make sure your eyes are saying exactly what you intend, let's look at a few basic guidelines for communicating with your eyes.

First, do your best to stay well rested so that your eyes do not appear to be bloodshot or glazed over. If your eyes are sluggish, others will perceive you to be sluggish. On the other hand, if your eyes are alert and alive, others will perceive you to be on top of things. Appearance does matter. I'm not talking about beauty; I'm talking about clarity.

Second, your eye contact should be direct, but not intrusive. For some, this distinction seems elementary, but to others, this is rocket science. I know a gentleman (he asked to remain anonymous), who suffers from a phobia known as Obsablepsia[2]. It is the nonability to look someone in the eye. He will be the first to tell you that he's struggled with clicking his entire life. People inherently distrust people who go out of their way to avoid eye contact. People think he's got something to hide. Even when he tries to force himself to make eye contact, it usually isn't direct, and he looks away too quickly, as if the eye contact has caused him great pain.

---

[2]Pronounced: OB-SE-BLEP-SIA.

Eye contact should be pupil to pupil when either you are talking directly to another person or they are talking directly to you. As painful as this might be, looking around the room, gazing at your feet, or looking at another part of their face will send the wrong message. Looking around the room will send the message that you are looking for someone perhaps more important to talk to. It makes the other person feel small and insignificant. I know someone who can't help himself from searching the room, even if he's in the middle of a one-on-one conversation. Gazing at the wall, your watch, or your feet sends the message that you bored or terribly distracted. You might as well yawn. Looking at another part of their anatomy will only make them feel self-conscious and preoccupied with what you might see. They might be wondering if part of lunch is still with them somehow. In any of these cases, the wrong kind of eye contact will definitely hinder clicking.

On the other extreme, too direct eye contact is not desired either. Eye contact should never be a penetrating stare if clicking is your goal. A terse stare might be the perfect gesture if you're in a boardroom negotiation or trying to get your teenager to clean their room. I know that when I am "negotiating" with my teenager, connecting is the furthest thing from my mind. Hard, penetrating stares can be effective communication tools, but it isn't recommended for building rapport.

But remember to follow their lead. If they reciprocate and appear comfortable with direct eye contact, so be it. However, if they appear uncomfortable and intermittently look away, then you should too.

SOUND

The second of the senses used to connect is sound. What we hear can be every bit as influential as what we see. I'm not talking about just any old sound, but particularly, the sound of your voice. *Paralinguistics* is the fancy term for the art of using your voice as a tool of persuasion. For years, I've been asking my audiences to name the top three things that contribute to building rapport. I get the usual answers, eye contact, handshake, and common interests, but rarely does anyone ever suggest the sound of the voice. I guess it's because it's one of those things that seem outside of anyone's control. After all, you can't change your voice, can you? I say you can, and you should if you want to click. You might not be able to change the basic tonality of your voice, but you can control rate of speech and inflection.

I could devote many chapters to this subject, but instead I will keep it concise and to the point. People primarily communicate in one of four vocal patterns. They are SRHI, FRLI, SRLI, and FRHI. I'll explain what each one means in a minute, but it's important to note that I am not talking about personality styles. Even though I am using four basic patterns as a means to identify communication styles, this is not intended as a labeling exercise. Unlike personality styles, we frequently move from one pattern to another depending on whom we're with, what we're doing, how we're feeling, and what's happening around us. This doesn't mean we're schizophrenic, just normal. It's not uncommon for someone to communicate in one pattern in one interaction, and a different pattern in another. The key is to recognize the pattern they're in at the moment and to follow their lead.

SRHI stands for slow rate, high inflection. People who communicate in this pattern speak with a relatively casual rate of speech and with a great deal of emotion and inflection. They are very expressive in their facial gestures and prefer to use people's first names. They tend to be good listeners and respond more favorably to open-ended questions, that is, questions that invoke a more detailed answer than simply a "yes" or "no." This is a friendly, warm, and informal pattern.

FRLI stands for fast rate, low inflection and is diametrically opposite of SRHI. People who are communicating in this pattern speak with a fast rate of speech and little or no inflection. They are monotone. This is often a pattern of power and decisiveness, and people tend to communicate this way when rushed, stressed, or trying to exert their authority. They have few facial gestures and prefer a more formal interaction. They respond better to closed-ended questions, that is, questions that can be answered in a word or very short phrase.

SRLI (as you've probably caught on) stands for slow rate, low inflection. People who communicate in this pattern speak with a deliberate, thoughtful rate of speech and little inflection. This is a pensive, detail-oriented, analytical pattern that often is mistaken for being aloof. People who are in this pattern tend to be skeptical and cynical of their surroundings, but once you've earned their trust, they warm up quickly. They prefer closed-ended questions and generally are uncomfortable with any physical contact.

FRHI communicators, fast rate high inflection, on the other hand, have no problem with physical contact as long as it is non-threatening. This is the most social, outgoing of the four patterns and is characterized with lots of facial animation and body language. They tend not to make the best listeners and can lose interest quickly if they are not engaged and having fun. This pattern is generally the easiest to recognize.

Let me reiterate: These are quick, general descriptions and not necessarily representational of someone's personality, but rather a snapshot of where they are at a given moment. Just because someone was SRHI in a previous interaction doesn't mean they'll be in the same pattern the next time. The power in clicking is to be sensitive and alert enough to quickly recognize what pattern someone is in and to follow their lead and communicate similarly. With a little practice, you'll be able to identify which pattern another person is communicating in within seconds and instinctively alter your pattern to match theirs. In my seminars, I often refer to this lightning fast adaptation as "rapport technology." The layman's definition of technology is a better way to do something, so it makes sense that if following their vocal lead is a better way to click, then it's a technology.

It's not so much a technology, however, to remember someone's name. While there are a few skills that can help, it mainly requires good old-fashioned desire and discipline. A person's name is the single-most influential word one can use in clicking. I'll never forget the time when the power of remembering a name became clear to me.

I've been going to the same dry cleaners for years, mainly out of habit and sheer convenience. They were the closest dry cleaners to my house. I was also convinced they were not the cheapest. On my way inside, I vowed that I would shop around next time for better prices. Then a funny thing happened. The familiar face appeared from behind the counter and without hesitation said, "Good morning, Mr. Rich. So good to see you again!" Wow. She knew my name. I asked her how she remembered or even knew my name in the first place. She smiled and replied, "I know the name of all my good customers." Makes sense to me. Needless to say, she's still my dry cleaner.

There's no magic to remembering a name, but there are a couple of rules to follow. First, of course, be sure to get their name. Ask. It's that simple. If you didn't hear it clearly or are unsure how to pronounce it, ask right away. When you meet someone new, there is a window of a few seconds when it's perfectly acceptable to ask about a person's name. If you don't seize the moment right away, the window closes and if you ask about their name later on, it can damage rapport.

The second rule is to use their name as soon as possible. The prevailing thought is that if you don't use it immediately, you will lose it. Our minds remember things clearer if we hear our mouths speak it, so using their name sooner rather than later is key to remembering it. We've all been in situations where we've forgotten someone's name and felt completely guilty or embarrassed, but that's nothing compared to what the person might be thinking. They might think they're not important to us, or that they must not have made a very good impression. They might feel disappointed, saddened, or even humiliated. Names are important. It's who we are, and one of the biggest ways to connect or disconnect.

TOUCH

Connecting through touch is sometimes referred to as kinesthetic communication. In more common terms, it's called touchy-feely. With some people, you increase the odds of connecting with them with an occasional casual touch, and by staying in close proximity. With others, you do the exact opposite. Proximity is the science of space and how people and objects relate to space. The three main types of proxemics are fixed space, semifixed space, and dynamic space.

Fixed space consists of objects that are largely immovable, such as walls, ceilings, trees, and cars. You can violate one's fixed space by entering someone's office unannounced or by cornering someone against a wall. Either will damage rapport.

Semifixed space consists of objects that can be easily moved, such as chairs, personal items, and paperwork. I recall a time when a brand new business acquaintance rode in my car for the very first time. He immediately started rifling through my CD collection and even thumbed through the armrest department. Thank goodness I had nothing to hide, but it made me uncomfortable and I even questioned his ethics. We never did business again. Moving or rearranging someone's semifixed space without permission can be a silent, but deadly, deterrent to rapport.

Lastly, dynamic space is human space. It is the space between people during communication. The general rule of thumb for Americans is to come no closer than an arm's length during a nonintimate encounter. Breaking this rule is a violation of one's personal space and should be done by invitation only. I can't help but recall the Seinfeld episode when Elaine's boyfriend was dubbed a "close talker." I remember the painful look of discomfort on Jerry's face when this "close-talker" came within an arm's length. He did his best not to back up or shy away as to not offend him. That was noble, but more commonly, our instincts take over and we unconsciously back up to maintain our distance. Be careful as to not offend them. [3] If you feel uncomfortable, try to move back slowly and casually so that your discomfort is not obvious to the other person. Moving away too

[3]Again, it's important to note that this book is written with American culture in mind. It is customary in many other cultures to communicate closer than I've written about here. In fact, backing up is even considered an insult in some cultures.

abruptly will only alert the other person that you've been uncomfortable and they'll be unconnectingly self-conscious from that point forward.[4]

How you move in space and what you touch can determine the quality of your clicking. As with sight and sound, it's best to follow their lead. If they communicate closer than an arm's length, consider it OK to reciprocate if you want. It's better, however, to always err on the side of caution, so if you're not sure of something, don't do it. It's great to be touchy-feely, but only with those who are also touchy-feely. Rapport is a fragile thing, and it's more easily damaged than it is established.

PUTTING SIGHT, SOUND, AND TOUCH TOGETHER

At the risk of getting too technical, sight, sound, and touch are interwoven and even sometimes at odds with each other. For instance, in addition to someone either communicating in one of the aforementioned patterns, a fifth letter can be added to the mix to create 12 possible communication patterns. An A (auditory), V (visual), or K (kinesthetic) can be added to SRHI to make someone SRHIA. This is slow rate, high inflection, auditory, and so on. Auditory communication is characterized by a recurring theme of sound. If someone ever says to you, "I hear what you're saying," chances are they are auditory communicators. If they say, "I see what you mean," then it's safe to conclude they are more visual. A simple, "I'm with you," or "I know how you feel," and bets are good they are kinesthetic communicators.

This might seem a bit too simplistic, but the implications to clicking are very real. Relationships can and do break down by not recognizing these simple truths and not following someone's lead. In

---

[4]I know "unconnectingly" is not a real word, but it works for me. Apologies to all English teachers who might be reading.

a marriage, if one spouse is auditory and the other not, they might forever complain that they never HEAR an "I love you." Conversely, the other spouse says, "Talk is cheap, I want to SEE your love." Then again, someone might just say, "Don't tell me or show me. I just need a hug." They simply wanted a TOUCH.

People want different things in their relationships. By recognizing, understanding, and complying with the desires of the other person, you will connect. It's connecting by choice, rather than by chance, and that's what clicking is all about!

Quick Click Tip

Clicking is a technology. It involves sight, sound, and touch. Start to notice the different ways people communicate and how they interact with you. A little psychology and a lot of common sense is the rule of connecting. Adapting your methods of communicating to their methods will go a long way. People will signal how to best click with them. The key is to pay attention.

6

Contagious Principle #4: Commitment

Oliver Wendell Holmes once said, "Man's mind, once stretched by a new idea, never regains its original dimensions." There is nothing more contagious than someone with an idea and the commitment to see it through. This kind of commitment is built through two ingredients: vision and voracity. Voracity is alternatively defined by the Webster's dictionary as a state of excessive eagerness. I love that definition. History is littered with stories of people who had a vision and the voracity to see it through. One without the other is lacking, but the two together form an unbeatable formula for success and are highly contagious.

People are drawn to people with commitment for two reasons. First, it is admirable. Very few people ever become truly committed to something. Small business failure rates are at all-time highs, divorce rates are well over 50 percent, college dropout rates are increasing, and very few people even make New Year's resolutions, let alone keep them. So when someone comes along who is committed to something, we take notice. At first, we admire them, but then our admiration turns hostile until we can determine whether their commitment is genuine or a passing fancy. Test this out for yourself. Announce to your coworkers your commitment to something. Their first reaction will be "good for you," then they'll proceed to tell you all the reasons why you can't, shouldn't, or won't do it. Once they see, however, that you are serious, true admiration is established.

The second reason why people are drawn to commitment is because we instinctively crave to fill the void that lack of commitment can cause. Despite all the data on our deteriorating state of commitment, we generally recognize it's not a good thing and aspire to be more committed. The world has gotten too vanilla. Political correctness has pulled everyone toward middle ground, and it has robbed us of strong beliefs once held. I understand why this occurred even if I don't agree with it. Spiritually speaking, silence has replaced prayer. Patriotically speaking, silence has replaced our Pledge of Allegiance, and politically speaking, silence has replaced having to choose between Republican and Democrat. Most Americans can't identify with either the extreme Right or the extreme Left, so we gravitate to the middle. Individualism is lost for fear of offending a single person. We play it safe instead of playing at all. It's all too vanilla for me. I'm not suggesting that we allow our beliefs to make war with those who disagree, just simply that we choose to disagree instead of compromising what we believe.

We fear alienation and disapproval, but interestingly enough, the exact opposite is more often the case. The funny truth is that people are drawn to people who know what they believe and don't vacillate in the breeze of public opinion. We admire leaders who are willing to stick their necks out and who are committed to their vision. Michael Douglas, playing the president of the United States in the movie *The American President* had a great line about this, he said, "In the absence of genuine leadership, people listen to anyone who'll step up to the mike." We're becoming vanilla by becoming void of real commitment. Country music's Aaron Tippin might have said it best when he sang, "You've got to stand for something, or you'll fall for anything." Vision gives you something to stand for; voracity keeps you from falling. Vision is the inward quality; voracity is what people see. Put the two together and your biggest concern about clicking is not if you can, but if you want to. You'll find yourself having to be selective with whom you want to click because *everyone* will want to click with you!

VISION

Most people think they have a vision, but they don't. Vision is not a fantasy blue-sky mental image that would take a genie's lamp to achieve. Sure, I'd like a palatial estate with sprawling acreage, horses, a couple of ponds, and a mountain view. Don't forget the helicopter pad to shuttle me to the nearest metropolis for fine dining. I can really picture this in my head. It's a nice fantasy, but it's not a good vision, even if it were attainable. That vision is universal. We'd all like that, but a vision must be about more than material possessions. It must be about making a positive contribution to society. If our vision is all about us, it won't be contagious.

Vision has two parts to it as well, purpose and mission. The two are often mistaken as being synonymous. Purpose is your reason for being. It's the part of your vision that drives the mission. It's what gets you out of bed in the morning. And there lies the problem. Most people don't have a purpose that drives them out of bed in the morning. Then again, most people aren't contagious either. The average person reluctantly gets out of bed in the morning only because they have to. It's time to go to work. The person who is committed to something can't wait to get out of bed. Think of purpose as the overall meaning for your existence and mission as your tangible goals. Individuals, as well as businesses, should not attempt to determine their goals and objectives until they are clear about their purpose. Purpose drives goals. Too often, businesses create elaborate mission statements that hang in their lobby and dispense goals to all employees, but upon further probing, no one bothered to clearly define a purpose. Vision is impossible to have without a purpose. Kevin McCarthy, author of *The On Purpose Person* and *The On Purpose Business*, believes a solid purpose statement should begin with the preamble, "We/I exist to serve by _____ (fill in your purpose here)." Once you've articulated your purpose, you're then ready to support your purpose by setting goals, the mission part of vision.

As with so many facets of these contagions, goal setting could be an entire volume in and of itself. While goal setting might only distantly be connected to outward rapport building, it is directly linked to commitment, which is a big factor in clicking. Goal setting is something everyone does, either deliberately or haphazardly. Haphazard goal setting is not premeditated. We know we've got some errands to run, but give no thought as to which errands to run first, second, and so on. Consequently, we spend twice as much time on the project and drive more miles than otherwise might be necessary. Nevertheless, we still set goals and complete the mission.

Haphazard goal setting is by far more common than deliberate goal setting, albeit the lazier of the two. Deliberate goal setting is premeditated and well defined. Deliberate goal setting not only aids us in being more productive, but it also keeps us motivated. It keeps us focused, on purpose, and is highly contagious. People want to be around people who know where they're going and have a plan for getting there. Although having clear goals can be a major factor in clicking, it is an essential part of any achievement. There's also more to it than meets the eye. I'm not going to get into the how-to's of goal setting; you can get that in a number of other places. I want to talk about four dynamics or truths behind goal setting that pertain to building your vision and your ability to click.

First, everyone knows about goal setting. It's been talked about forever. There are countless books, tapes, videos, and seminars on the subject. It's preached in schools, hospitals, churches, governments, and commerce. Kids as young as four years old know about New Year's resolutions, and I've read recently that as many as half the adult population in America have had a goal to lose weight at some point in their life. Goal setting is part of our culture, and it's not rocket science. It's generally seen as something anyone can do at any time.

Which leads us to the second truth: Very few people do. I'm not talking about the occasional goal or haphazard goal setting; I'm talking about regular, consistent goal setting. Very few people do. This is precisely why it's so contagious. You've probably heard the saying that more people plan what they're going to eat for lunch than plan what they're going to do with their life. My own informal survey in my community showed that less than one in four adults had a specific vision for their future.[1] Sure, people have vague ambitions, but goal setting is specific. Everything worthwhile requires specifics. Anyone can be a generalist, but very few people become experts in something. It's this specific preciseness that people instinctively admire. To see something with a clear, specific vision of what they want to accomplish is nothing short of awe-inspiring.

Thirdly, your goal must be your own. If you've ever worked in sales, you've probably been given a quota. A quota is a sales goal that must be met to either gain a reward or in some cases, continue employment. Many companies do this to set benchmarks and to motivate their sales people to do better. I won't debate the philosophy of quotas at this time, but suffice it to say, fear is only a short-term motivator. The point I want to argue is the definition of a quota as a goal. Quotas might be the goal of the company, but until it becomes the goal of the individual sales person, it's just a number. A goal that you don't have any emotional connection to can't be defined as your own. Goals should be highly personal things. If you're in a position where a goal is thrust upon you, it would be very wise to either adopt it as your own or negotiate with your employer for one you can adopt. Otherwise, the odds of hitting it decrease.

---

[1] I asked 49 people over the course of a weekend if they had specific goals for the next five years, and only 9 people answered with a definitive yes. Many more said they had plans (haphazard goal setting), but nothing specific.

The beautiful thing about goal setting is that results are inevitable. It's simple cause and effect. Those who set clear, specific goals regularly achieve more than those who don't. There are tons of research to support this claim, but none as strong as common sense. Knowing where you're going is key to getting there. The impact on clicking is an obvious one. People who achieve more command greater respect and admiration.

Everyone loves a winner. We're a nation that is obsessed with fame, fortune, and power. Our entire system of capitalism is built to reward achievement. Clicking becomes easier when people seek to first click with you. Michael Jordan not only has more opportunities to click than the average Joe, but his ability to click is enhanced as well. In normal circumstances when two people meet, there are two sides trying to evaluate each other. In Michael Jordan's case, most people want to click with him so intensely that they've already decided to do so before even meeting him. The only real evaluation going on is on his part. Now, I know what you're thinking, this is a superficial level of clicking and you're right. I don't know Michael Jordan, but I'd speculate that it's hard for others to truly click with him because of less than genuine motives. The implication is clear. Those who have clear, specific goals achieve more, and those who achieve more have one less barrier to overcome when meeting new people, and that's the barrier of credibility. Of course, the more you click, the more successful you become, so it's one never-ending cycle, and it often starts with having goals.

The last dynamic of goal setting is that it begins in the mind. It is mental. Before anything exists in physical form, it must first originate in someone's mind. This ability to imagine things that are not yet created is where goal setting begins. You can't write down a goal you can't imagine. For instance, if you can't close your eyes and see yourself 25 pounds lighter, then it's no use making it a goal. The ability to mentally see your *vision* (the greater the detail, the better) is the difference between a pipe dream and a deliberate goal. I call this "visioning." Visioning is essential and is incredibly contagious in that being able to articulate and describe your vision is what enlists others to your cause. If you can't see it, they can't either.

One of the most incredible people of the twentieth century was Walt Disney. Did you know a newspaper editor in Kansas City once fired him because he couldn't come up with any new ideas? Boy, did he have the last laugh! Imagine meeting a broke, dejected Walt Disney at the precise moment he came up with the vision for Disney World. He must have been really good at it because lots of people became infected with his idea. His vision clicked, which, in turn, made him click with all the people who helped make Disney World a reality.

How do you know if your vision is capable of this kind of contagiousness? Answer: You'll know. It's all in the way you perceive your goals. If your goal is a goal because it "would be nice," then it will never be contagious. Remember earlier in this section when I said your vision must contribute something positive to the world? This is vital if your vision is going to tap into synchronicity.[2] Your vision must become more than a mere goal; it must become your calling.

I'll never forget the day my speaking career started to really take off. For some, I know it's hard to pinpoint the exact moment, but I knew. I woke up one morning after only a couple hours of restless sleep consumed with worry about whether or not I could continue with my vision of being a full-time professional speaker. Bills were mounting and I didn't have enough business on the books to make it through that week, let alone the month or year. I wrestled all night long with the thought of taking what my mother called, "a real job." Then, as if the light of day inspired the light inside me, I woke to the realization that I simply could not do anything else. I didn't have a choice. This is who I am. It is my calling. I made a pledge to myself that morning that for better or for worse, sickness or health, richer or poorer, I was in this business for life. My vision became my calling

---

[2]See Chapter 2 for more on synchronicity.

and I made the commitment to never look back. Did this mean I didn't continue to struggle? No, the struggles got worse before they got better. My world didn't change immediately. What was different, however, was inside me. I was committed. (Which is ironic, because some thought I should be "committed," if you know what I mean.)

Ask yourself these simple questions. First, do you have a vision? Second, is it yours or someone else's? Lastly, has it become a calling? When your vision becomes a calling, you become contagious, not to mention voracious!

VORACITY

Voracity completes the journey to rock-solid commitment. Voracity is the outward manifestation of vision and is most commonly used to describe one's eating habits, but I like Webster's second definition: excessive eagerness. It's good to be eager, but what does it mean to be excessively eager? Eagerness is being excited with the anticipation of something you desire. Excessive eagerness, I believe, slips into sheer drive and blind determination. Excessive might mean eager beyond all imagination and logical reason. Voracity is not logical; it's emotional. It's wanting something so badly, you're consumed by it. It's the ultimate display of commitment. Allow me to share a few shining examples of voracity.

F.W. Woolworth, the man some call the "father of the convenience store," was employed as a youngster at a local dry goods store. He was not allowed to wait on customers because the owner didn't believe he knew anything about the retail business. F.W. left to strike out on his own.

Beethoven loved music. He was given the gift of music that few have ever known. Tired of playing other composers' music, he started writing his own despite having been told by his music teacher that he was, and I quote, "Hopeless as a composer."

Thomas Edison was an inquisitive boy. I can't help but think he'd be labeled with ADD today. A grade-school teacher told him he "was too stupid to learn anything." Martin Luther King, Jr. was reprimanded time after time for lacking emotion when he spoke in front of his junior-high-school class. Michael Jordan was cut from his tenth-grade basketball team. Louis Pasteur was rated mediocre in chemistry by his professors at the Royal College and was told to find another passion. Rico Caruso's very first music teacher told him to give up singing. The list is endless. Thank God they were voracious. Their visions were their calling, and giving up wasn't an option.

It would be nice if there were a magic pill that we could take that would give us this kind of drive and determination, and instantly make our visions our calling, but there isn't. It, as with all contagions, starts inside before it's apparent outside. There are, however, two outward things you can do to help facilitate inward change.

First, practice the Law of Scarcity. This law[3] says that people value things more if they believe they are scarce. Think of the Cabbage Patch Dolls or Furby dolls. They were illogically expensive and very hard to get. People waited in lines as trucks were unloaded for the opportunity to maybe be able to purchase one. They were scarce. This same dynamic can work for you too. Simply always have someplace to go and something to do. It's best if you really do, but if not, creating the illusion of scarcity is just as effective.

People who are committed to something are movers and shakers, and movers and shakers always have something to do. I'm not advocating blowing people off and cutting conversations short, which would be contrary to the very premise of this book. I am saying though that it's best to end every interaction leaving them wanting more than to linger uncomfortably and leave them with the impression that you've got nothing going on.

Again, I remember a *Seinfeld* episode where George adopted the law of scarcity, though it didn't call it as such. He decided to abruptly end every conversation on a high note. When another person laughed

---

[3]OK, it's not a municipal law or anything, but rather a law of human dynamics. Besides, it sounds good.

at something funny or witty he said, he immediately said, "That's all folks," and exited the scene. OK, this is a bit extreme, but what did you expect from George? Scarcity works. Businesses use it all the time, why not you?

Second, dedicate yourself to knowledge. Knowledge is the fuel of commitment. The more you learn about something, the more naturally committed you become to it. We can even lose our commitment to our calling if we stop learning and become stagnant. I can test your level of commitment by asking one simple question. What book is currently on your nightstand? Based on the responses I get in my presentations, I know that some of you haven't had a book there in years. Others only have magazines and *TV Guide*. Some have a book by Danielle Steele or John Grisham. Hey, I'm a huge Grisham fan. I think he's the best fiction writer of our generation, but those are leisure books, not books to inspire commitment. Grisham is great Saturday afternoon reading, or down by the pool, or in an airplane, but not right before bed. That last 10 minutes before going to sleep should be reserved for reading something inspirational and developmental.

I read once that the average person falls to sleep at night watching television, more specifically, watching the news. I was a journalism major in college, and journalists have a motto: If it bleeds, it leads. That means that if there is blood involved, it's a lead story on the news. It's gross, but it's all about creating shock to get ratings. There's nothing more negative than today's news. So, if you're like me and must tune in to at least get an idea of what's happening, do it earlier in the evening and not right before bed. Our brains don't shut off. They continue to process information and thoughts. If you feed your mind with negative stuff, you will wake up unrested and sluggish. Reading something positive and inspirational will ensure a better night's sleep and keep you focused and committed to your vision. Nothing speaks to your level of commitment louder than your commitment to learning. If you can create the habit of learning for just 15 minutes each night before bed, your level of commitment in all phases of your life will increase.

I also love asking about learning whenever I get a chance to interview people. I ask them to name the last three books they've read. If you can't do it, or it's been too long for them to remember, I don't hire them. My rationale is simple, if they're not committed to themselves, why should they ask someone else to be committed to them? Knowledge fuels commitment and is one of the greatest gifts you can give yourself.

Commitment is not easy, but then again, nothing worthwhile ever is. I started this chapter with a quote, so why not end it that way as well? Dr. Martin Luther King, Jr. captured the core of commitment when he said, "If a man hasn't discovered something that he will die for, he isn't fit to live." Well, that might be a bit harsh, but they certainly will be ill-equipped to click!

Quick Click Tip

Very few people ever develop the kind of commitment to something that causes others to stop and notice. If you've never bothered to commit your goals to paper, now's a good time. Write down everything you'd like to accomplish in your lifetime. Then break them down into short-term, intermediate, and long-term. Cross off anything that doesn't truly get you excited and get your heart pounding with anticipation. Then tell everyone who'll listen. Declaring your vision to the world has a profound way of making it come true.

7

Contagious Principle #5: Conviction

Conviction is my personal favorite contagion. Even the sound of the word is contagious. As I look back on the people in my life that I was naturally drawn to, the one common denominator was conviction.

Conviction is in the same family as commitment, but with a different focus. Commitment comes from the head; conviction comes from the heart. Commitment leads to conviction, which is why it follows it in this book. In fact, all the contagions work in harmony with each other. They're all interwoven and interrelated and come together when you click with others. Conviction can only occur if you are committed to something. You can have commitment and still lack deep conviction, but not the other way around. You can't have conviction without commitment.

Conviction is defined as a strong belief in something, and I certainly concur. However, to be a major contagion, we'll need to define exactly what those strong beliefs are. The three components of conviction are passion, optimism, and principle. I remember it by their initials, POP. Passion and optimism are outward qualities, and principle is an inward quality. Unlike the previous contagions, I'll start with the outward qualities of conviction first. The most visible one is passion.

PASSION

Passion is to life what flavor is to food. Passion is a natural extension of commitment and is the root element of conviction. Where conviction is strong and deep, there is passion. Passion is one of the most misunderstood qualities of life. Passion is often viewed as an extreme emotion. It's OK to be excited about something, but strong passion is a bit radical. I've talked about why this is so in an earlier chapter. Passion is a natural human state. We're born hard-wired for passion, but somewhere along the way, we gradually are conditioned to temper our passion. Then one day we wake up and realize that passion is to life what flavor is to food and spend time, money, and energy trying to get it back. Passion makes everything we do more rewarding. I learned the lesson of the importance of passion the hard way.

I mentioned earlier that ever since I was a little boy, my mother told me I'd be one of two things when I grew up: a salesperson or a preacher. So, naturally, when I accepted my first full-time job as an adult as a salesperson, I knew it would be a breeze. After all, I had the natural gifts to succeed in selling. My mother told me so. So you can imagine my shock when after six months my boss called me into his office and gave me "the speech." The "speech" went something like this, "David, you have all the natural talent and ability you need to be successful, but you lack something even more important, passion." And he fired me! It couldn't be. How could I get fired from selling, my predestined career? It was a blow to my ego, but I quickly recovered and became my next company's leading salesperson and eventually started my own business as a speaker.

In 1995, when my first book was published, *How to Stay Motivated on a Daily Basis!,* I sent a first-edition copy to my first boss who fired me. I signed it with a huge "Thank You!" in big, bold letters. He taught me, albeit the hard way, that talent is fine and dandy, but without passion, it means nothing. I didn't understand the meaning of James Barrie's immortal words, "The secret of happiness is not doing what one likes, but in liking what one does."[1] I wasn't committed to my job and therefore lacked the passion that a demanding job like selling requires. Sales people need to develop passion to sustain them through the inevitable rejection that comes with selling. Most sales people never make the commitment to their profession and consequently become discouraged too easily.

Without a genuine commitment, passion isn't passion. You might get excited from time to time, but it isn't real passion, so it all begins with commitment. But it doesn't end there. Once you're truly committed, you'll need to cultivate passion. Without passion, even the strongest commitment will eventually begin to erode. That's exactly what happened to me. But it only happened once. I learned how to cultivate and tap into my natural passion, and it's made a difference in every aspect of my life. With passion my marriage became stronger, my career was more rewarding, my spiritual life was reawakened, and my physical and mental state improved. The secret truth behind passion is that it must come first. Passion always precedes the accomplishment. Passion is an inflammatory condition. Whatever you get passionate about will expand and swell. Passion is contagious, but you need to have it before you can infect others with it.

There's lots of ways to increase your passion level. I've written about one in the last chapter: knowledge. A continuing dedication to learning can and will increase your passion for whatever you are committed to learning about. Hopefully, I've already convinced you that knowledge is power. Health is a factor in passion. Poor health saps your energy, and low energy equals low passion. You don't need to be a triathlete or run marathons, but you do need to take care of your body. You can be the best racecar driver in the world, but if you're in a broken down car, you'll never win.

---

[1]James Barrie wrote *Peter Pan*. As you've probably already deduced, I love the great quotes. This book is sprinkled with some of my all-time favorites.

Then there is the passion builder I frequently refer to as "SOMA Power." I'll explain exactly what that is in a minute, but its roots are in the "Act As If" technique.

Acting as if is not new. It's been the subject of many books and mentioned in countless others. Its most common description is "Fake it till you make it." It simply means that you can act something into being. For example, if you "act" happy long enough, you'll eventually become happy. If you act as if you are passionate, the world will see you as passionate, and in time, you'll actually BE passionate. We are the sum of what we repeatedly do. Changing our life is as simple as creating new habits.

It's written that 21 days is the habit-forming or habit-breaking time frame. If you do something, or don't do something, for 21 days in a row, you can either create or break an existing habit. I believe this holds true for passion as well. If you "act" passionate for 21 days, you just might find that you won't need to act quite as much. You'll have conditioned your body to be passionate. That's where Soma Power comes in.

SOMAPSYCHOTICS

You're familiar with the term psychosomatics, I'm sure. It's commonly thought of as an imaginary illness or condition, but that's not accurate. A psychosomatic condition is a real condition; there's nothing imaginary about it. The root word "psycho" is Greek for mind, and "soma" is the Greek word for body. Psychosomatic simply means mind first, body second. It's psychosomatic when something starts in the mind and then moves to the body. Have you ever said to someone, "I feel like I might be coming down with something?" That's psychosomatic. How about, "I know I'm going to be tired tomorrow." Psychosomatic again.

If you stop and think about it, almost everything we do is psychosomatic. We wait until our minds give our bodies permission to act. We laugh only if our minds thought it was funny; we lash out if our minds are burdened; we cry if our minds think of sad things. It's almost exclusively mind first, body second.

But what if we could turn it around? Instead of psychosomatic, we'd be somapsychotic, which is body first, mind second. Instead of waiting for our minds to give permission to our body, we act first. Weak is the person whose thoughts control their actions; strong is the person whose actions control their thoughts. We can change the way we think by taking action. The very act of acting passionate can lead us to genuine passion.

Not taking action and allowing our thoughts, moods, and emotions to reign supreme will rob us not only of passion, but many other contagions as well. It is my contention that this is precisely the reason why most adults live less passionately than kids. Kids don't overthink. They take action. They don't wait until good happens before they allow their passion to be known. They're passionate first, and their bodies display it readily. I've marveled at the sheer excitement my youngest son gets at the mere mention of a trip to Baskin-Robbins. His passion is natural and it always precedes the event. I, on the other hand, am thinking his reaction is absurd. It's only an ice cream cone for goodness sakes. Adults, psychosomatically, wait until our minds rationalize, overthink, and conclude that it's OK to get excited about something. Talk about absurd. It's not as if our minds are beacons of positive thinking.

Most of our psycho-overthought is negative anyway. The fact is, we can change our state of emotion simply by taking physical action. When I'm feeling low on energy and maybe even a bit depressed, I sometimes stop, drop, and do ten push-ups. It's amazing the rush of energy I get just from getting my heart pounding and blood flowing. That's somapsychotic. I didn't feel like moving, much less doing push-ups, but I did it anyway. It never ceases to change my emotional state, albeit just for a short time, but that's all that's needed most of the time. So take some kind of action right now. Try this. Let out a loud "YES," start clapping and do the "Arsenio" thing.[2] You might think that sounds ridiculous, but do it anyway. See if you start to feel a bit different. I'll bet you will. Then you can tell your friends, you're a somapsychotic!

OPTIMISM

Now that we know how to control our emotions by action, it's time to supplement that with the power of positive thinking. You can't jump up and down forever. Pretty soon, you'll get tired and you'll be left with your thoughts. Only you can determine whether this is a good thing or a bad thing. I've known people who'd go to great lengths to avoid being by themselves because it was such a lonely experience. Is life a blessing or something to be endured? Are people generally good or bad? Is the glass half full or half empty? Questions such as these underline our thinking. Optimism is an essential ingredient to sustaining our conviction both inwardly and outwardly.

Very simply put, people go out of their way to be around people who are optimistic and avoid pessimists like the plague. *Optimism is hope in action.* Optimism is nothing more than expecting the best and believing in good, and without hope there can be no optimism. Hope is the most precious of all contagion qualities. I am so thankful that in the many times of my life when I needed a dose of hope and a shoulder to cry on, I had an optimist to call on. An optimist isn't interested in dispensing advice on what went wrong; they only want to uplift and edify. They believe, deep down, that no matter how gloomy things look at the time, tomorrow will always be better. This is more than just a rah-rah feel-good thing. It's a basic truth of life. If you expect the best, that's often exactly what you'll get. Flip Wilson used to say (I'm showing my age), "What you see is what you get!" The mantra of optimism is very similar: What you expect is what you

---

[2] I'm referring to the hoot and holler that Arsenio Hall's audiences would do to begin each show. It's been off the air for years now, but that's what most people remember about his show.

get. Hope for good things and good things will happen; hope for bad things and bad things will happen. This is optimism in a nutshell. This, of course, is easier said than done.

Optimism is not like shaking hands. It's not easily mastered. There's even some evidence that it is genetic, something you're either born with or not. Some researchers believe there is an optimism gene! While this might be true, being born without the gene should not be an excuse for negative thinking. Optimism is something you can learn. It's a little-known secret, but optimism is unquestionably a learned trait and there's now good reason to learn it. Researchers at the Mayo Clinic studied 450 people starting in the 1960s and have just concluded a recent follow-up. They found that people who were optimistic lived longer and were more physically and mentally fit than those who weren't!

Three factors play a significant role in learned optimism: childhood development, mental dialogue, and belief in abundance.

The way we learn as children goes a long way in determining optimism. If we grew up in a positive, encouraging environment, chances are high that we'll be optimistic adults. This seems fairly obvious. But what is less obvious is how children are taught to handle difficulties. Researchers now believe that problem-solving and coping skills are vital components in cultivating optimism. If children don't learn how to figure things out on their own and to cope with adversity, even the happiest children might become pessimistic when faced with a major challenge. Researchers Stewart Page and Kathryn Lafreniere cite the following example. When a child is stuck at the top of a tree, shouting for help, most parents' first reaction is to climb the tree and get the child down immediately. Rescue might be simplest for children, but it teaches them dependence on external sources. On the other hand, parents should resist rescue and instead encourage the children to patiently make their way down themselves by communicating the expectation not of, "I'll save you," but rather, "You can do it yourself." And later, instead of saying, "You're now safe with mom and dad," one might say, "I knew you could do it." By teaching children to solve their own problems and to cope with the process, they will grow up optimistic and confident in their ability to navigate through rough waters. Encouragement is ultimately more effective than instruction.

Along the same lines, parents should not be quick to assign fault to everyday problems. Researchers with the Penn Optimism Program (POP) at the University of Pennsylvania found that optimists see problems as something outside of themselves, while pessimists tend to believe that problems are always their fault. This is not denial or problem avoidance, but rather an acknowledgment that problems can happen to anyone, anytime, and assigning fault won't do a thing to change it. I'll talk about this again later in another chapter. By focusing on what to do rather than whose at fault, we can stay empowered and encouraged, and in turn, more optimistic.

There is such a thing, however, as reckless optimism. This kind of optimism by all costs is anything but contagious. People avoid reckless optimists. Martin Seligman, author of *Learned Optimism* says that there are definite times when optimism is inappropriate. He says that when the cost of failure outweighs the cost of success, optimism should be tempered with common sense. He uses the example of an airline pilot debating whether or not to de-ice the plane in questionable weather. In this case, because the cost might be fatal, it's better to think of the worst-case scenario, rather than be recklessly optimistic. However, even taking this extra cautionary measure can ultimately still be optimistic. It's because you value life and believe the best is yet to come that you take this action. Suicide bombers wouldn't give a second thought about de-icing!

Mental dialogue is self-communication. It's the things we say to ourselves. When you stop and think about it, we talk to ourselves more than anyone else. In its most basic sense, we need to learn how to click with ourselves before we can ever expect to click with others.

Unfortunately, much of our mental dialogue is less than positive. I've read reports speculating that as much as three-quarters of mental dialogue is negative. I'm not sure any study can be definitive when it comes to thinking, but I can use myself as a barometer. I'm a fairly positive person. I make my living teaching and preaching on motivation and success, yet all too often I catch myself engaging in negative mental dialogue. Maybe not three-quarters, but too much for my liking. Before you say you're glad you're not me, let's define what constitutes as negative self-talk. The following is but a partial list: self-doubt, pity, condemnation, worry, regret, blame, envy, remorse, comparison, anger, jealousy, hatred, guilt, and fear. Imagine having someone follow you around all day whispering negative things in your ear. I'll bet you wouldn't last more than a single hour before you told that person to get lost. Yet we readily accept it from ourselves. Like any habit, you can reverse the cycle. You won't be able to completely rid yourself of all negativity, but you can tip the scales so that it's overwhelmingly positive.

You can do this by replacing a negative thought with a positive one. Whenever you think something negative, tell yourself to shut up. Have a little mental argument. Tell yourself that you won't tolerate that kind of thinking and offer a positive alternative. Go back and forth until the positive wins. If for some reason the negative wins, concede that round and vow to win the next. Say to yourself, "OK, you might have won that one, but you won't get me!" Think of the negative as not being the real you. You are positive and optimistic, even though an occasional thought or two is negative. Too often we see ourselves as negative with an occasional positive thought. Murphy's Law taught us this concept. Don't buy it. Problems will happen, and negative thoughts will creep in. Fight through them. Winning is simply getting up one more time than falling. Charles Kettering once said, "The only time you can't afford to fail is the last time you try." Winning the battle of your thoughts is one of the hardest things you'll do, but also the most rewarding. You'll click with others to the exact degree you click with yourself. You are the product of your thoughts!

The third and final factor in optimism is abundance, or rather your view of abundance or lack thereof. Abundance thinking believes that there will always be enough to go around and that you'll always get what you need. It might not always be what you want, but always what you need. Your needs will be met.

Paul Zane Pilzer wrote a phenomenal book on the concepts of abundance and scarcity called *Unlimited Wealth*. He points out that abundance believes resources are unlimited, regardless of how it might seem at the time. A perfect example is the gas shortage of the 1970s. I remember it well. By law, you were only allowed to buy gasoline on the odd or even day corresponding to the last number of your license plate. If your plate ended in an odd number, you could only buy gasoline on an odd-numbered day, and you had to buy at least five dollars worth. Topping off an almost full tank was against the law. Lines of almost a mile long were not unusual. Getting gas was a half-day's work! All this because gasoline was deemed to be in short supply. It was scarce. I recall reports predicting that if we continued to use oil and gasoline at the current rates, we would exhaust the world's supply in fewer than 20 years.

Well, 25 years later with double the usage, we're in good shape. Since the 1970s, we've built the Alaskan Pipeline, and increased technology has allowed us to drill deeper and in places we couldn't before. Distribution has become more efficient, and with the end of the Cold War, we have access to places we didn't have access to in the 1970s. Oil and gasoline weren't scarce, only our ability to find it.

Same is true with life. Optimists believe in abundance. They believe that despite their current situation, things can change in an instant. Opportunities can present themselves overnight, and people can come into our lives that we didn't even know about. We live in an abundant world where the glass is always full. It might appear half empty because that's all our eyes can see. The truth is it's always full. Optimism is hope in action, or in other words, having faith in favorable outcomes. Combine encouragement, positive mental dialogue, and a belief in abundance and you'll be the biggest optimist anyone will ever meet!

PRINCIPLE

Rounding out the qualities of conviction is principle. It's the inward quality that makes the outward qualities of passion and optimism possible. We live in a world all too void of principle and absolute truth. It is impossible to click with conviction if you lack principle. Principle is defined by Webster's as a general truth or fundamental law. It's believing in something so deeply it defies logic. It's not facts that matter; it's the principle (or truth) that matters.

As I write this, we are still engaging the enemy in Iraq. Regardless of where you stand on the merits of the war, one has to admire the courage and principle of British Prime Minister Tony Blair. At one point, more than 80 percent of his constituents were against the war, but he never wavered. His political future and power were on the line, but that didn't matter. Thanks to C-Span, I watched as he all but told members of Parliament that if they voted against the war it would be without Tony Blair. It was principle that mattered. Some might say the same of President Bush, but Bush never faced the overwhelming opposition that Blair faced. At least not in the beginning. For weeks, I had a hard time putting my finger on exactly why I liked him so much, but it eventually became clear. Blair's principle was contagious. He believed that war was the right thing to do and convinced his country he was right. It was a study in clicking through principle. Only time will tell whether he actually was right, but it won't change my admiration for him. He'll always be a man of principle to me.

A less dramatic example of principle is my daughter's belief in Santa Claus. She's now a teenager and wouldn't be caught dead on Santa's lap anymore, but I recall a time when she was seven years old that best illustrates the principle of uncompromising belief. We were on our way home from a Christmas Eve church service, just daddy and daughter. Mommy was home trying to wrap presents and get two younger brothers to bed. To kill a bit of time, we drove around looking at Christmas decorations when suddenly we both saw something we'll never forget. We saw Santa! There he was, creeping around the side of a neighbor's house in full red regalia and sack slung over his shoulder to boot. Her eyes lit up. She was convinced she just saw something no other kid alive had ever seen.

If you were to have tried to convince her that there was no such thing, she wouldn't have believed you. She just would have thought you were crazy. She saw the man and he was real. Her belief in Santa was so strong that we decided to tell her rather than risk her future mistrust. After all, she was going into eighth grade and might have faced ridicule if we hadn't come clean. Principle led us to divulge the truth and it was principle that caused her to hang on to the myth. Whatever you believe with all your heart becomes your reality. Santa was her reality even though he didn't exist in physical form. That's why you need to be clear as to what you believe. The dynamics of principle doesn't distinguish right or wrong, fact or fiction, truth or lie, but it does determine your level of conviction.

Conviction is a strong thing. Those who have it seem to possess an inner magnet that is not easily or logically explained. You believe in something and you're willing to show it. Conviction multiplies the armies of rapport. Andrew Jackson might have said it best, "One man with conviction makes a majority."

Quick Click Tip

Conviction is passionate, positive energy that flows out of you and into the world. People with positive energy attract lines of people wanting to just hang around. Rid yourself of all negative thought by play-acting the part of an overly positive, optimistic person. Give yourself 21 days for the experiment. If a negative activity is the norm, do the opposite. Spring out of bed in the morning. Let bad news bounce off you. Smile at everyone. Others who know you will think you've gone mad, but that's OK. After all, you're just acting soma-psychotically. Don't be alarmed as time goes on if you find yourself acting less and less!

8

Contagious Principle #6: Cheerfulness

If there were such a thing as a self-explanatory contagion, it would be cheerfulness. It stands to reason that cheerful people click better with others than noncheerful people. Most people would define cheerfulness as being pleasant, but when it comes to clicking, cheerfulness means a whole lot more. It's a deeper quality than merely putting on a smiley face. That reminds me of the countless customer service departments I've come across that try to mandate cheerfulness by placing mirrors at their rep's desks to remind them to smile. On the surface this sounds like a novel idea, but once the novelty wears off, the mirrors are unceremoniously tossed aside.

Real cheerfulness doesn't need a reminder, and it's exhibited inside out, not outside in. Cheerfulness is as much a state of mind as it is a way of acting. Cheerfulness is like clicking in miniature. Clickable people click. Cheerful people naturally act cheerful. Miserable people act miserably. Behavior is the result of who you are. One can act cheerful in any given moment of time and still not BE a cheerful person. Conversely, a cheerful person can have moments of not being so cheerful. The moral of the story is clear, however. Cheerfulness is contagious. We all want to be around people who not just act cheerful, but actually are cheerful.

Cheerfulness starts inside, but I want to work backward. I'll start by talking about the outward qualities and end with the inner. Cheerfulness rubs off. It's a lot like selling. If you're excited about your product or service, chances are good that will rub off on your customer. So, for that reason I give you an easy way to remember the qualities of cheerfulness: SELL. The letters S, E, L, L, stand for the qualities that make up clicking cheerfulness.

SMILE

A smile is often referred to as universal communication. In any language, in any country, in any culture, we know what a smile means. It's the ultimate outward signal of cheerfulness. A single smile can say more than a hundred words. It has been known to ease tension, clinch a sale, ignite a romance, convey thankfulness, create loyalty, invite intimacy, and open doors.

A smile just might be the single most important nonverbal gesture. And anyone can do it! The ability to smile is something we're born with. It's free, easy to do, and no equipment or assembly is needed. So why is it that we don't smile more? Well, that might be a whole other book, but one explanation might be that too often we're told not to smile. I've experienced and witnessed mothers and fathers commanding their children to "Wipe that smile from your face, young man!" Expressions such as "This is no laughing matter" and "It's nothing to smile about" are part of our everyday language. Smiling has become so scarce that if we do it for more than 30 seconds, our face muscles hurt. Take the test. Smile as big as you can for 30 seconds. If your muscles feel stretched or there's even the slightest ache, you might suffer from "smile depravity." You're not alone. No one smiles as much as they should.

I'm tempted as of this writing to inject a story or two to illustrate the power and importance of smiling, but I've decided to trust

CREATE EXCITEMENT: BE A SMILE GIVER!

that you already realize that. The questions then become how can we get others to smile more readily at us, and is there a good way or a bad way to smile? These are more pertinent to clicking.

Getting others to smile is not as hard you might think. It doesn't involve telling a joke, standing on your head, or making funny sounds. It's simple reciprocity, or otherwise known as, "What goes around, comes around." You receive back what you put out. So, naturally, the best and quickest way to get people to smile at you is to first smile at them. Smile and the world smiles back. It's simple, and the dynamic involved has been much studied, but you can test this yourself very easily.

Next time you walk down the street or through a mall, smile and make eye contact with people as you pass them by. If your results match clinical studies, an overwhelming majority of people you smile at will smile back. Also note that you'll be strangely aware of more smiles than ever before. It's as if we didn't notice smiles before. You'll also notice the return smile you give to those who beat you to the punch. The power of reciprocity is immense. When someone does something nice to us, we feel indebted to return the favor. When someone takes you to lunch, we feel like we must at some point return the kind deed. Sometimes it's out of guilt, other times out of sheer decency, but whatever the motive, we almost always reciprocate.

Smiles are no exception to the dynamic. The only difference in smiling is that it's usually subconscious. Owing someone a lunch is one thing, but rarely does someone think about owing someone a smile. This proves the innateness of a smile. It's already there; it just takes someone smiling at us to awaken the smile within. So, I ask you, are you a smile giver or a smile taker? Smile givers are proactive clickers, while smile takers are passive. I'd bet that by the mere fact that you're reading this book, you want to be proactive, so be a smile giver. It's nothing more than a habit. Smiling can open doors to new people and new opportunities that will change your life. Think about this one; every significant relationship you have first began with a

HEEEEEEEEEEEEEEY!

smile. It's the starting block of clicking, but it's not just for meeting new people. Smiling is a beginning, but it's also a sustainer.

There might not be a good or bad way to smile per se, but there is a way to employ a smile that can yield tremendous results. I call it the "Big Greeting," a kind super smile. It's a way of greeting someone that I actually learned from my daughter. If she ever entered a beauty pageant, she'd win Miss Congeniality hands down. Whenever someone approaches her to say hello, she reacts as if she's known that person all her life. Her eyes light up, her voice softens, she smiles, and greets them with enough energy to power a small city. It makes no difference whether she knows them well or can't even remember their name. If they know her, they get the "Big Greeting." What's amazing to me about this is not that she does this, but how she is received. It seems logical to conclude that a greeting such as this would be met with trepidation, but that's not the case. They respond in kind. I'm not sure whether it's another case for reciprocity or a case for emotional ambush, but it works. It instantly breaks down any walls of communication and creates an intimacy that otherwise might take much longer. It's a way of taking "Good to see you" to new heights. It's an amazing clicking tactic, but I sense it's not merely a tactic to her. She feels it in her heart, and others sense that. It's a physical transference of cheerfulness, and it places the interaction 10 paces further down the path of rapport than it otherwise might have been. It's a smile on steroids. Recommended dosage: Each time you see a familiar face, smile!

ENCOURAGEMENT

If a smile is a rare jewel, encouragement is the Hope Diamond. Encouraging words are the fuel of cheerfulness. A "big greeting" can get an interaction off on the right foot, but the wrong words out of your mouth will break it. Words have a way of impacting others long after you've left their company. William Hazlitt, a nineteenth-century English writer, once wrote, "Words are the only things that last forever." I can attest to that. I can barely remember what I had for dinner last night, but I remember the words of my high-school track coach some 25 years ago like it was yesterday.

My three relay partners and I were sitting in the infield warming up for our race at a very big track meet. Our coach came out to see if we were ready. He very nonchalantly told us he had extreme confidence in us because after all, and I quote, "We were the four best runners in the entire school." Now I knew the other three were great runners, and for him to include me with them was a compliment in the highest regard. I still hear his voice to this day.

Mine is not an isolated case. You remember the words, "I have a dream," and "Give me liberty or give me death!" Do you remember who said them? OK, those were easy. How about the words, "Taxation without representation is tyranny," or "Business is business," or "Ignorance is bliss?" Do you remember who said them?[1] Probably not. Those words have long outlived the people who said them. That's the power of words. They are permanent. They stick in our hearts and minds and continue to affect us forever. Some words affect us for good, while some devastate us. Words can either uplift or tear down. Clicking words are encouraging, uplifting words. Clicking words are confident and optimistic. They leave the other person feeling better for their interaction with us. A person who is able to leave every encounter knowing their words encouraged the other person will never have a "clicking" issue.

So just what kinds of words are encouraging and uplifting? The answer is twofold. One is obvious, the other not so. The obvious answer is compliments. Everyone likes to be complimented. The catch is to make sure it is a genuine compliment and not cheap flattery. People can spot an insincere compliment from a mile away.

---

[1]The "taxation" quote was from American Patriot James Otis. "Business" quote is from a French playwright named Octave Mirbeau, and the famous "Ignorance" quote is from English poet William Langland.

There is a proper way to compliment, and clickers know it. A compliment should be immediate and nonthreatening.

I've read that the average person thinks to himself or herself something genuinely nice about another person at least 33 times a day, yet only verbalizes 3. That's less than 10 percent! I have no clue how one can measure such thoughts, but the exact number isn't important. What is important to note is (whatever the number) we aren't quick to share our good thoughts with others. We do just the opposite. Too often, we're quick to point out flaws and share negative thoughts, but hold our tongue on the nice thoughts.

This is a major difference for people who click. Clickers say the good and hold back the bad. Again, I'm not talking about making up nice things to say; I'm merely suggesting we share a nice thought when we genuinely think it. And we shouldn't wait. The less time between the thought and the compliment, the more sincere it is perceived. If we wait to say something, we risk the perception of having ulterior motives. Time to think about saying something nice diminishes the impact of the compliment. A sincere compliment should come from the heart, not the head.

We should also avoid complimenting a physical feature unless it is someone with whom we have a very close relationship. The rule of thumb is never compliment a physical feature unless you are within the intimate communication zone. You should remember that from the chapter on Connectedness. Instead, compliment an action or an emotion you feel as a result of their action or physical feature. It's not always appropriate to tell someone they've got beautiful hair, but it is OK to say that their hair makes you jealous, or you wish you had their hair. This is less threatening and is generally viewed as being more sincere.

Please note, however, that common sense must reign. Not every felt emotion makes for a good compliment. Some things are indeed better left unsaid.

The other category of encouraging words is what I call, "*contagious talk*." Contagious talk is nothing more than communicating the contagions and avoiding "woe" talk. If people want woe, they can get their fill from the nightly news. People want contagious talk. For example, it is encouraging to people to hear others speak with humility, passion, vision, and wonder. It is positive communication at its best. I have a friend that occasionally calls me up just to ask me if I saw the sunset or to tell me about a flower she saw on the side of the road. I laugh at her trivialness at times, but she is always uplifting to talk to. I know someone else who is the embodiment of humility. He does so much for others, yet he is always giving the thanks and praise to someone else. I am encouraged to be a better person every time we talk. I could go on and on, but you get the picture. Contagious talk is uplifting and edifying and always leaves the other person a bit better than they were before. Try it sometime. The amazing thing is that not only will you encourage others, but you'll be encouraged too. You can't spread contagious talk without it affecting you as well. It's the magic of encouragement!

LAUGHTER

Laughter is an extension of smiling, but it very well might be the most contagious quality one can possess. I say possess because while anyone can physically laugh, it's the people who have developed a sense of humor who are the most contagious. Some experts have even developed tests to determine a person's humor quotient. Some of my very best speaker friends make a good living speaking on nothing but the power of humor.

Humor is a powerful tool not only in clicking, but also for peak physical performance. I don't want to get too medical or scientific, but this much is known about the physical effects of laughter. When we feel stress, our bodies release a psycho-neuro chemical into our blood streams called corticosteroids, which is then converted to cortisol, which is referred to by doctors as a stress hormone. Cortisol, in elevated levels is known to suppress our immune system. Laughter, along with other endorphin-raising activities, has been proven to lower cortisol levels and thus helps the body stay healthy and disease free.

In a recent article in *USA Today*,[2] cardiologist Jerome Fleg of the National Heart, Lung and Blood Institute reported that happy people might be less likely to produce stress hormones that make the blood stickier, thicker, and prevent coronary arteries from dilating easily. In the same article, cardiologist Beverly Brummett of Duke University Medical Center, conducted a study of 866 adults with heart disease for 11 years beginning with an initial questionnaire about how much joy and happiness they had in their lives.

Her results were astonishing. She reported to the American Psychosomatic Society that cheerful people had a 20 percent better survival rate than that of noncheerful people. She even took into account key factors such as severity of their condition and if they smoked. The article went on to say that joyful people might enjoy higher levels of emotional support from friends and family, and according to psychiatrist Steven Locke of Harvard Medical School, "They are more likely to get it because of the kind of people they are." Internist Mary Whooley of the Veterans Administration Medical Center in San Francisco added, "Unhappy, isolated people may be less inclined to take their medications, to eat healthfully, or to exercise." Further proving the connection between emotion, joy, and laughter to physical health. Not to mention, unhappy, noncheerful people are way less likely to click.

OK, there you have it. That's as scientific as I get, but this is really no laughing matter. My best friend is a doctor (and a darn good one at that), and he tells me that there are hospitals across the country that specialize in treating disease with laughter. Patch Adams is not fiction. Laughter can heal. Amazingly enough, it can also be a powerful business tool, and one I'll write more about in an upcoming chapter.

Now consider this, if laughter is known to have powerful effects on the body, how much more powerful is it to clicking? I have a

---

[2]I didn't save the date of the article, although it was early 2003 and was written by Mary Elias for the Life section of the paper.

theory. This one isn't scientific or proven in any extensive study, but I believe it's true nonetheless. I profess that if two people share a laugh within the first two minutes of meeting each other, they will inevitably click. It's my "two-minute laugh rule." Laughing binds the souls together quicker than any other single factor. Don't ask me how it works, it just my theory, but test it for yourself. I invite you to share your results with me. I'd love to include a few proven testimonials in my next book. Besides, even if my theory does not always lead to instant rapport, you'll be a healthier person!

LOVE

Rounding out the last element of cheerful (and the final "L" in my S.E.L.L. acronym) is the strongest of all contagion qualities, and that is love. To steal a line from the Beatles, "All you need is love." They might not have been talking about clicking, but it's probably the shortest piece of profound wisdom I've ever come across. Love sums up what it is to always smile, encourage others, laugh easily, and otherwise be a shining example of cheerfulness.

I'll never forget the time a major corporation brought me in to analyze and speak to their customer service staff. Loyalty was slipping and they believed it had something to do with service. They were right, but service wasn't the root; it was lack of love. That might sound bizarre in a business reference, but that's exactly what it was. In my silent observation I overheard a few "key" employees lamenting on how disruptive clients can be. I even heard one person say something that nearly knocked me off my chair. She said, "I could get a whole lot more work done if customers would stop bugging me!" I couldn't believe it, but I found the problem. Thanks to a less-than-cheerful attitude coming from the department head, the staff had grown to see customers as an interruption of their work. Their boss was close to retirement and had grown cynical and had a misguided notion that a boss should never let his or her employees see you smile. He lost his love for his job and certainly didn't have any love for those pesky customers.

If you suffer from a lost love for your fellow man, take comfort in knowing you can reclaim it. It starts with always looking for the positive in any situation and in any person. Every single person has something uniquely positive about them. It might be buried under years of trial and tribulation, but it's there. Make it your mission to decipher people's gifts (remember the section about gifts in Chapter 3), and to let them know you see it. They'll appreciate the compliment, and you'll feel better for having made someone else feel better. That's love in action. We all have it; it's simply of matter of use.

Love might seem completely oversimplistic and abstract, especially after writing about the scientific data on laughter, but if the shoe fits, I have to write about it. You need to have a love for people for it to even be possible to click to everyone every time. Love isn't something you pull off a shelf when you need it. You must have it to share it.

Love has many degrees and is present to some degree in every clicking interaction. Love might not be ALL you need in ALL things, but you'll never be contagiously cheerful without it. You can fool some people some of the time with a painted-on smile, but you can never fool yourself. Besides, eventually even others will see through the paint. With love, however, you won't ever need the paint. Your smile, encouragement, and laughter will simply be signs of the love you have inside!

Quick Click Tip

Cheerful is as cheerful does. Here are a few suggestions. Smile at complete strangers on the street as you pass by. Pay the toll for the car behind you. Leave a note of encouragement for someone. Bring a coworker a soda. Compliment at least two people every day. Hug your spouse and kids for no particular reason. Every act of cheerfulness brings a return of tenfold. The wheels of synchronicity have been set in motion. You might not always see your return of investment, but you'll know it in your heart.

9

Contagious Principle #7: Courage

The cowardly lion was a very likable creature. Just think how contagious he'd have been if he had only had courage! Courage is the noblest of all contagions, but let's set the record straight. Courage is not just for wars, climbing Mount Everest, and walking down a dark alley alone at night. Courage is needed every day. If you've ever navigated the highways in some of our big cities, you know exactly what I mean.

Almost everyone in business needs daily courage. Moms and dads need courage to stick to their guns in raising children. Kids need courage to stand up to bullies. So many everyday things require courage. Someone once told me that the most terrifying moment they ever had was when they left their customary seat at church to go down front to be introduced as a new member. For most, that would be no big deal, but to some, it's a monumental act of courage.

Of all the quotes in this book, Teddy Roosevelt's is my absolute favorite. He said,

> The credit belongs to the man who is actually in the arena, whose
> face is marred by dust and sweat and blood; who strives valiantly;

AWESOME QUOTE!

who errs and comes short again and again, who knows the great enthusiasms, the great devotions, and spends himself in a worthy cause; who at the best, knows the triumph of high achievement; and who at the worst, if he fails, at least fails while daring greatly, so that his place shall never be with those cold and timid souls who know neither victory nor defeat.

I love many things about that quote, but what I love most is the call for courage. One can argue that in these modern times, we live in a leadership vacuum. That is, leaders are few and far between. While there are many aspects of being a leader, the chief quality is courage. You need courage to lead, and leaders take action. It doesn't matter if you win or lose, but just that you've tried. Not trying leads to the fate that Roosevelt spoke of, dying with those who know neither victory nor defeat. This fate, however, can be avoided, but it takes (you guessed it) courage.

Courage is a unique contagion in that the inward and outward qualities are identical. They manifest themselves from different perspectives, but they are the same. They are action, uniqueness, and persistence. It's a good chicken-or-egg question to ask which leads to which. Does taking action, being unique, and sticking to your guns give you courage, or does courage enable you to take action, be unique, and stick to it? The answer is both. Some might be born predisposed for courage, but for most, it's something we learn, by taking action!

ACTION

Have you noticed that courage is usually referred to as an ACT of courage? That's because courage isn't courage without an action. Then again, the same can be said of all the contagions. The subtle difference, however, is that courage is *solely* defined by action. One can be confident but never display it. It might not do any good not to display it if you have it, especially for clicking, but it's theoretically possible. It's not possible, on the other hand, to be courageous and not have it displayed through action. Courage is defined by an act of courage. You might think courageously, and that's noble, but it's only through action that it becomes true courage, and true courage is contagious!

Now some will argue that a person dying of a terminal condition is courageous, and to that I say, they could be. But there needs to be some kind of action taken. Acceptance should not be mistaken for courage. Acceptance is a part of contentment and that can be contagious as well, but it's not courageous. I'll tackle the contagion of contentment in a future chapter. Courage needs an act.

We admire courage. As I've stated earlier, it's the noblest of all contagions. We all aspire to act with courage in those moments when it's called for, and most of us think we will. The truth is, though, we can never be sure. Action has its enemies: fear, complacency, and excuses.

Fear is a very real emotion, and it often gets the best of us. Fear displays itself in a number of ways. Fear can be outright trepidation. That's the fear of horror movies. However, more commonly, fear is displayed in less obvious ways like indecision or excessive worrying. These conditions are known as "contagion busters." OK, maybe they're only known as such by me, but that's exactly what they are. For example, I wrote about the powerful contagion of commitment and goal setting in Chapter 6, but working against commitment and courage is worrying. Worrying is nothing more than negative goal setting. The same dynamics are involved. I wrote about the contagion of conviction in Chapter 7, but working against conviction and courage is indecision. Indecision paralyzes a person, and the result is inaction. There's no courage in inaction. You've probably heard the truth that a person rarely regrets the things they did, but rather the things they did NOT do. Action is the only cure for fear and indecision.

Complacency robs us of creativity and the need to be courageous. We're all creatures of routine. Think about your morning ritual. Chances are, you do the exact same things every day, the same way, in the same order. The problem is that when we unconsciously go about our business routinely, we often miss opportunities to shine and act with courage. We end up seeing only the things we expect to see and only trying the things we know how to do. Life becomes nothing more than a routine. No courage necessary. We don't take any action because we simply didn't recognize the need. We're living on autopilot. No pain, no gain, no risk, no glory, no action, no courage.

Excuses, on the other hand, are usually in response to a recognized opportunity, but we uncourageously pass. Every day, we all face one or two moments when we think about doing something we know deep in our hearts we should do, but we usually end up talking ourselves out of taking action. We convince ourselves that we're too busy, or too broke, or too old, too young, too inexperienced, too out of shape, or that it just isn't the right time. The argument might have some merit, but more often than not, fear was somehow to blame. It might be for fear of change, fear of the unknown, or fear of risk or failure. Fear is capable of preventing any act of courage. In those moments, we must employ "contagioustalk"[1] to overcome our excuses and just do it. I'm convinced that Nike became so successful not because they made a great pair of sneakers, but because they popularized the phrase "Just do it." We all want to just do something. No one is exempt. This, of course, had a contagious effect on their sales.

In those moments, if we can muster the courage and take action, people will line up to applaud. We live in hero-less times. It's harder than ever to quickly think of three people we admire enough to call hero. I have a theory on this. It isn't because of a lack of heroes, but rather because of a lack of hero coverage. Villains sell. To prove this, try to quickly name three people who became infamous for their wickedness. That's easy. It's hard to stop at just three. The media is quick is deliver bad news, while good news gets pushed to the "we'll get to it if we can" pile. I know first hand. I was journalism major in college, where I first heard of the old adage, "If it bleeds, it leads."

---

[1] Refer to the previous chapter for more info on "Contagioustalk."

Which means, if there's blood involved, it's lead story material. Sad, but true. The truth is there are plenty of good news and stories of everyday courage out there. We might have to dig a little, but it's well worth it. Stories of courage inspire us and will help us find our own strength and courage when we need it. So, to do my part, I'd like to share the following stories that came my way not too long ago. They inspired me, and I hope they will you too.

ACTING WITH COURAGE

You've heard of Chicago's O'Hare Airport, but you probably aren't familiar with the story behind Butch O'Hare. Butch was a World War II fighter pilot in the South Pacific. It was February 20, 1942. During one of his many missions, he noticed that someone had forgotten to refuel his aircraft, and he didn't have enough fuel to complete the mission with the rest of his squad. His commander ordered him to drop out of formation and head back to the base for fueling.

On his way back he noticed something that caused his heart to skip a beat. A fleet of enemy bombers was heading toward his comrades. He knew they were not prepared to engage the enemy, and worse, he had no way to alert them of the impending danger. It was a moment of truth. He could take action or regret it for the rest of his life. Throwing caution to the wind, he dove into the heart of the formation of Japanese planes. He dove in and out of their formation, causing as much disruption and distraction as he could. He even dared to get close enough to attempt to clip off an enemy wing or tail to disable their craft. Despite being hit repeatedly by gunfire, he didn't let up until the Japanese squadron abandoned their mission and took off in another direction.

Butch was barely able to land his badly damaged plane, but he did. The camera mounted on his plane told his tale. He had been able to destroy five enemy aircraft and became the first Naval Aviator to win the Congressional Medal of Honor. A year later he was killed on another mission.

Years earlier in a seemingly unrelated story, there was man nick-named Easy Eddie. He was Al Capone's lawyer. He was personally responsible for keeping Capone out of jail with his legal prowess. As a result, he was paid very well. He lived the high life despite the atroc-ity that surrounded him. He also tried hard to shield his son from the escapades of his infamous boss. Eddie's conscience caused him to work extra hard at teaching his son right from wrong. As his son grew older, Eddie could no longer hide the reality of his job from him. He had a decision to make. It was his moment of truth. Trembling,he went to the authorities and agreed to testify against The Mob. He knew what that meant, but he was determined to set the right example for his son. A few months later, Eddie was gunned down on a Chicago side street as retribution for his betrayal of Capone.

What do these stories have in common? Two things. First, they are real stories of ordinary people who acted courageously in their moments of truth. Second, Butch O'Hare was Easy Eddie's son.

Talk about synchronicity! I believe these acts of courage were connected. Eddie's act was meant to lead to Butch's act. One act of courage almost precipitates another.

2) UNIQUENESS

The equation works like this: Uniqueness is contagious, which leads to clicking, and you need courage to be unique. Got it? People with courage take action, and one form of courageous action is to proclaim your uniqueness. In other words, it often takes courage to be you. Everyone wants to be someone else. Why not just be you? There's nothing contagious about conformity, but it takes courage to step out from behind the sea of conformity.

We live in a world where we're taught to conform. There are countless routines that one goes through every day, not as a result of logical thought, but rather because it's the way we see others do it. We learn by watching others. I call this, "followership." It's the essential opposite of leadership. It's the systematic method of learning to follow.

I've mentioned that I make my living speaking and consulting to corporate America. Companies bring me in to effect some kind of change. This requires that I ask a lot of questions. I'd be a wealthy man if I had a nickel for every time someone told me the reason they do something the way they do is because "that's the way it's always been done."

Followership is gradual. It starts out harmless enough, but eventually we lose all ability to imagine things differently. It usually begins in childhood as a stern warning against being different. A label, such as troublemaker, class clown, disrupter, contrarion, or simply someone who steps out of line, often follows. We then learn that to be different is a bad thing. We're told to be like everyone else. Even adult ad campaigns exhort us to "Be Like Mike." Followership is perfected and cemented in our subconscious in middle school. It's the ideal training ground for the herd mentality that will be with us forever.

Most middle-school children would rather lose a finger than do anything to stand out. It might be from lack of confidence, or perhaps, a fear of being mocked, but conformity is a religion. The argument of the day becomes "everyone is doing it." Forget whether it's right or wrong, the only thing that matters is being like everyone else. Individuality is replaced with running with the pack. With few exceptions, they want to wear the same clothes, like the same music, eat the same foods, watch the same movies, and do the same things. Fortunately, this wears off a bit by high school, but for most, the damage is done. We've formed opinions, thought patterns, and habits that keep us in bondage to conformity. Unless we recognize this condition and do something to snap ourselves out of it, we become subject to becoming one of those cold and timid souls who know neither victory nor defeat. We die vanilla. Sameness is a disease and is a huge obstacle to overcome.

The ironic thing is that the very same things that get us labeled in childhood are the very same things that potentially can make us great as adults. Our unique gifts (discussed in Chapter 3) are too often not recognized as gifts. Fortunately I had a mother who saw my penchant for talking too much in class as a "gift of gab." I wasn't encouraged to talk, but I wasn't chastised either. It was my gift. Someone who asks a lot of questions shouldn't be told not to. It might be their gift. The same is true for the kid who gives away her lunch (Mother Theresa), or the kid who reads instead of playing at recess (Albert Einstein), or the kid who sings in the lunchroom (Brittany Spears). Gifts not seen as gifts become repressed, and the opportunity for greatness lost. We become Jane and John Does. Kids who don't "act" like everyone else must need medication. Let's suppress his or her energy and uniqueness until everyone is alike. Unfortunately, this too often is the worst thing for children, not just in damage to self-esteem, but also in failing to recognize their uniqueness.

In business, the fastest way to success is through the things that make a business unique. It's no different with individuals. Discovering our uniqueness and having the courage to display it is the fastest way to individual success. Not to mention, it's incredibly contagious!

3) PERSISTENCE

Probably the best pure sales person I ever met was a fellow named Joe Walsh.[2] He mentored me in a little yellow pages' venture back in the early 1980s. His greatest sales qualities were his passion for the business and his persistence. He simply never gave up. He didn't have a college degree, didn't come from a wealthy family, and didn't get that one big, lucky break. He just worked hard and didn't quit.

I have so many Joe Walsh stories (I know he cringes at the thought), but the one that stands out the most was the time we made

---

[2] Not the Joe Walsh of the Eagles rock-and-roll fame.

a sales call to a florist in Bethesda, Maryland. We walked into the shop and upon learning we sold yellow pages, the owner immediately told us to "get out!" I don't recall the exact words, but it was something to the effect that he wouldn't care if he saw another yellow pages rep for the rest of his life. We walked out disappointed, but went on about our business. The next day, we were back in the same area and Joe wanted to revisit our florist friend. I thought he had finally flipped his lid. I did my best to talk him out of it, but I lost. I sheepishly followed him into the shop.

He strode, as if on a mission, right up to the counter and made the following proclamation: "We stopped by yesterday to introduce the merits of advertising in our directory when an unpleasant creature yelled at us and told us to get out and never come back. We never got a chance to tell anyone why our directory is so great. That creature isn't still here, is he?" I inched toward the door; certain the owner's next move was to call the police. I was far too young to go to jail! To my amazement, after what seemed like a solid minute of uncomfortable silence, the owner cracked a smile and invited us into his office.

Needless to say, we emerged with a new customer. I was in awe. I asked Joe how he knew to go back into that shop so soon after being rejected. His answer has stuck with me for more than 20 years now. He told me he didn't know if the timing was right to go back in, but he was willing to take a chance. He went on to say that selling is all about timing. Just because someone says "NO" today doesn't mean it will be a "NO" tomorrow. Something in the florist's demeanor told Joe that he was just having a bad day and another day might be different. If Joe had given up (as so many sales people do), we not only wouldn't have made that sale, but I wouldn't have learned a lesson in persistence. Today, Joe is President of Yellow Book USA, the nation's largest independent yellow pages company!

It takes courage to be persistent. It's easy just to give up. I am firmly convinced that most people give up not realizing how close they were to succeeding. Legendary football coach Vince Lombardi once said, "The difference between a successful person and others is not a lack of strength, not a lack of knowledge, but rather a lack of will." He was right. Joe Walsh wasn't contagious because of his strength or knowledge. In fact, he only has a high-school diploma. Joe was contagious because he had the courage to "go for it." Courage completes the puzzle for many of the contagions. It's great to have confidence, but you need courage to take action. It's great to have commitment, but you still need to act on that commitment. Even cheerfulness requires courage sometimes.

Sometimes it takes courage to smile in the face of adversity and conflict. The greatest courage, however, is the courage to be you, and only you. Resist the temptation to be like someone else. The ironic truth is that if you try too hard to get someone to like you and to be something you're not, it backfires. If you try too hard to click, you will clash. Just be you, and never stop being you. Obstacles will jump into your path and challenges will persist, but you must persist even more. By taking action, celebrating your uniqueness, and being persistent, you will develop the courage to lead and click. The world will always line up to applaud courage. It's an all-too-rare contagion.

Andrew Jackson once said, "One man with courage makes a majority." To put it another way, acting with courage will be extremely persuasive! Click. Click.

Quick Click Tip

Never pass on an opportunity to be bold. Every day we're faced with decisions on whether or not to take some kind of action or to take the easier road and do nothing. By choosing to ACT, even with the small, seemingly insignificant activities, we will slowly build the habit of acting courageously. Courage is choosing to act. That is the essence of leadership. If you fail, so what? There's always tomorrow. But there will never be another today. People rarely regret the things they did, but rather the things they did not do!

10

Contagious Principle #8: Competency

I can't tell you how many times I have felt a genuine connection with other people and really looked forward to getting to know them better, only to have it evaporate in an instant because of their lack of competency. There is an undeniable link between competency and true rapport. The world loves a winner indeed. But what exactly is a winner, and what makes someone competent?

The answer is not an easy one because it is so subjective, but I define competency as being capable, trustworthy, and together. Being capable is largely outward. It's the part of competency people can see. Trustworthiness is both inward and outward. It starts with the inward quality of integrity and displays itself outwardly with reliability. Togetherness is mostly inward. One might appear outwardly together, but it's merely a mirage if one isn't together inside. You need all three to have the kind of competency that clicks with others. It's a package deal. The catch is that it's completely in the eye of the beholder. Let me explain.

BEING CAPABLE

What one person deems as capable, another might condemn. Being capable might mean being accurate, or being a fast worker, or both. While it's a tough one to definitively define, the outward quality of being capable almost always means a job well done, whatever that might mean to you. Being capable is all about perception, knowledge, and effort. Let's start with perception.

If someone perceives you as being capable, then you are. Conversely, if someone perceives you as being incapable, you are incapable to that person. The facts are irrelevant. You might be able to make a case for your capabilities, but the only thing that matters is how you are perceived. Perception is reality.

Let me give you a few examples.

My dishwasher died last summer and in my house, this was an emergency. Of course, it was a Saturday, so finding a repairman home and available was no easy chore. After calling a half dozen numbers, I struck gold. The gentleman I reached said he "was on his way." Three hours later, he arrived. He appeared disheveled, unorganized, and his shirt was inside out. Three times he had to go back to his truck because he grabbed the wrong tool. He dropped a screw, which proceeded to roll under the fridge. Finally, I had enough. I had as much confidence in his capabilities to fix my dishwasher as I did my own, and that's pretty darn low. I told him that I decided to wait until Monday and shop for a new one. I didn't, of course. It was a little white lie, but I figured that was better than telling him I thought he was incompetent. The truth is, maybe he wasn't. Maybe he was just a bit clumsy, or having a bad day. Either way, it didn't matter. The only opinion that mattered was mine.

This sounds harsh, but things like this are an everyday occurrence. How about hanging up on a company's representative because you didn't like the tone of the greeting, or throwing away a piece of mail solicitation because it wasn't aesthetically appealing? How about changing your mind about a dinner special because the server couldn't tell you about it, or avoiding a certain teller in the bank line? We all go out of our way to interact with people we perceive to be capable and avoid those we don't.

Let's break down my experience. First, he showed up later than I expected. Although he didn't specify an exact time, he led me to believe he was coming right over. My perception was that his capabilities were already affected by his tardiness. Second, his appearance was less than professional. Not that I was expecting something out of a *GQ* magazine, but I was expecting neat and clean. Appearance matters! You certainly don't need to wear the finest clothes. Just wear what you got, the best you can. Lastly, he made a couple mistakes by grabbing for the wrong tool and dropping a screw. These errors, by themselves, might not have doomed the relationship, but coupled with the other contagion busters, he had no chance. I had deemed him incapable, and we were not going to click.

The second part of being capable is sharing your knowledge. I don't know if it would have been enough for my dishwasher guy, but it would have been nice if he explained what he was attempting to do and why. Information helps build perception of competence. You might be confident in what you're doing, but sharing knowledge lets others feel confident about you. Seeing a doctor is a good analogy. Doctors who are good at keeping their patients informed cultivate patients who have total faith in their doctors. As patients, we feel empowered by information and are skeptical with lack of information. The subtle truth here is that sharing knowledge will not only work for doctors, but you too. It empowers people, and that helps you click!

An industry that is definitely not clicking with customers these days is the airline industry, and it's not hard to figure out why. Recently I was on a plane that landed late in Dallas, and just as we were minutes from the gate, the Captain announced that another aircraft was still occupying the gate so we'd have to wait. The whole plane groaned because it was late at night and we were already over an hour past our scheduled arrival time, but he assured us it would be "no more than 30 minutes." Well, as you've probably suspected, it wasn't 30 minutes. An hour and 10 minutes later, we pulled into our gate. Now, I want to be fair about this. The Captain was at the mercy of airport traffic control. I'm sure there was nothing he could do to get us into the gate any sooner, but he could have kept us informed. With every 30 minutes, his restless passengers became more and more agitated. Keeping us informed would have eased our anxiety a bit and would have shown his concern. Instead, he chose silence. He obviously didn't care about clicking!

When sharing knowledge, it's important to not just share the who, what, where, and when. The most crucial is the why. Sharing the why is the most empowering. It's the difference between training and education that I wrote about in Chapter 2. Training tells someone what to do, but education tells them why to do it. This is one of the most common mistakes in business today. Education empowers, while training degrades. This truth isn't only for business. For instance: Telling your spouse and children WHY you love them is more powerful than the "I love you" itself. Also, telling your employees or coworkers WHY you appreciate them is more powerful than the quick pat on the back. Not that pats on the back and "I love you's" aren't important; they are. I'm merely suggesting an even stronger alternative. Going the extra step and sharing the why will increase the connection tenfold.

The third and final piece of the capable puzzle is effort. You've heard the expression that the proof is in the pudding, well, the proof of being capable is in results, and all results begin with effort. People respect genuine effort. The popular phrase says that "It's the thought that counts," but what really counts is effort. A thought with no effort is of no value, but when I couple a nice thought with some kind of effort, then it has meaning. The phrase is really talking about effort, regardless of the outcome. As long as you've tried, that's what matters. We tell this to our kids all the time. Do your best. Put in the effort. Then, if you don't get good grades, so be it. We can live with effort. It's when we don't put in the effort and just settle for mediocrity that is damaging. Unfortunately, too many people settle for doing what's easy and make excuses for their lack of effort.

One of my favorite clients is a Director of Sales named Trish. I love being around her. Her energy is contagious. Everyone loves Trish. (Sounds like a TV show.) The thing I admire most is that she is solidly driven by effort and results. However, that wasn't always the case. For years, she allowed her sales team to swoon her with excuses and mediocre performance. She liked them, so she let them get away with it. With a little coaching, and a nudge or two from her boss, she came to realize that results were the only thing that mattered. She needed more effort. She thought this tough new outlook would jeopardize her relationships, but the exact opposite happened. It strengthened them. For the first time, her sales team knew exactly what she expected and what the consequences would be. They responded by working harder than they ever had, and results followed. Trish respected and appreciated her team's effort, and they clicked like never before.

Effort always leads to greater competency, and that almost always leads to greater rapport. Effort is the most visible thing for others to judge us by. We can hide feelings, but we can't hide effort. It's out there for the whole world to see. Sometimes people even test our effort to determine whether they even want a relationship with us in the first place. One such thing happened to me years ago.

It was early in my speaking career and I had been trying to get an appointment with this particular client for many months. Finally, my persistence paid off and he agreed to see me the next day at six o'clock. I thanked him and in my closing remarks said, "I look forward to seeing you tomorrow evening at six!" He immediately corrected me. He said he didn't mean 6:00 P.M.; he meant 6:00 A.M.! I gulped, said, "See you then," and hung up. An appointment at 6:00 AM was no small task. I lived in Northern Virginia and he was in Washington, DC and that meant leaving my house no later than 4:45 AM to make sure I made it on time and to find parking. Not to mention, it was February and I had to allow time to scrape my windshield and warm up my car. My day would begin at 3:30 A.M., and needless to say, this was long before my day usually begins. As I was driving to the appointment, I couldn't help but think of what I might be capable of doing should this all be a cruel joke or if he stood me up, but thankfully, that didn't happen. We had a great meeting, and by 7:00 A.M., he had signed a contract to do business with me. I was on a high leaving his building and recall thinking, "Now what?" I was finished with my first sales call before I was normally awake! But it was a good feeling. The bigger reward, however, was not the contract, but the words of wisdom he forever left me with. He told me that he always sets first appointments for 6:00 A.M. He said he was legitimately busy and at that time he could focus without interruption, but it was what he said next that stuck with me. He said that if a sales person hems and haws, or suggests another time, he wouldn't see them. They blew their chance. His logic was sound. He said that if a sales person weren't willing to go the extra mile to MAKE a sale, they assuredly wouldn't go the extra mile once the sale has been made. It was a lesson in effort I'll never forget.

TRUSTWORTHINESS

This one sounds so obvious. If someone doesn't trust you, you probably have no chance to click. While this is true, trust is more often created and/or broken in the little things as opposed to the big things. Telling people outright lies or stealing from them are surefire ways to damage trust, but so is exaggeration or simply not keeping your word. Trust leads to respect, and without respect, clicking is out of the question.

I personally believe that trust is at an all-time low, especially among businesses and the buying public. Recent corporate scandals certainly have not helped. The good news is that trust is finally getting the attention it deserves. Look at the rash of universities that have fired sports coaches because of violations in personal conduct. Some might cry foul, but when trust is broken, the relationship can never be the same.

Trust begins inside. It begins with having integrity. Integrity means that you are personally governed by doing the right thing. It means not only keeping the letter of the law, but the spirit of the law as well. It means that just because you might not have outright lied, you still might not have told the truth. Trust is a delicate thing and one that doesn't take into consideration loopholes and technicalities. Its only concern is what is right. Pleading ignorance is no excuse. Trust has many components, but the main two are keeping your word, and acting ethically.

I recall a time earlier in my career when a client had inadvertently sent me a duplicate check for my speaking fee. I knew their accounting department was a mess and it would have been extremely easy for me to keep the money. If and when they ever found out, I knew their disarray could be used against them. I needed the money. My career was too new and I had mouths to feed. I actually contemplated keeping the money, but I didn't. Even if I had gotten away with it with my client, my conscience would have convicted me hard. I also knew that though I could plead miscommunication, it would have damaged the relationship. They might or might not have believed me, and the risk was not worth taking.

What happened next shocked me. I sent back the money with a note thanking them for their faith in me, but paying me twice wasn't necessary. They immediately sent it back, also with a note, saying they appreciated my trustworthiness and asked me to apply the additional payment to a future program! They instantly became one of my favorite clients, referring me to many more clients through the years. The moral of the story, however, is unmistakable. If I had not acted ethically, our relationship wouldn't have been as strong. Trust is the ultimate act of competence and is absolutely crucial to clicking.

Keeping your word is a major part of trust and is every bit as important. It's too easy to say something and then rationalize about it later. In customer service circles, there is a well-known adage that is excellent advice to live by: "It is better to underpromise and overdeliver, than to overpromise and underdeliver." It's all too common to say something in the moment to appease someone only to have it get lost in the shuffle later. Nothing will kill rapport faster than a broken promise.

On the other hand, nothing builds trust faster and perception of competency faster than keeping your word, no matter how small or insignificant it might seem. If you say you're going to do something, do it. It sounds so elementary, but when it comes right down to it, trust is a rare commodity. It's not that people's intentions are to deceive. I believe we say things fully intending to keep our word. But then we get busy. Things come up. Life gets in the way and before we know it, our plans are foiled. It happens. We hope people understand, and for the most part, they do. However, we must also realize its impact on clicking. Rapport takes a hit each and every time our word is not kept. It's like a bank account. Every time we don't keep our word, a withdrawal is made. Each time we do, a deposit is made. The catch is that the withdrawals are always at least four times the amount of the deposit. Depending on your balance, a single withdrawal can wipe you out. So too can a broken promise.

Now, I guess it's important to note that a promise doesn't have to include the actual label. My kids think that if they say something and don't do it, they're OK as long as they don't "promise" it. They think they've found a loophole. However, they are wrong. As I've stated earlier, loopholes and technicalities have no bearing on trust. It's a black-and-white issue. There's no room for error. Trust is either 100 percent or it's nothing at all. You can't trust someone 75 percent of the time, or even 99 percent of the time. You never know when that 1 percent will hurt you. It will always be in the back of your mind.

Trust feeds competency. The more trustworthy you are, the more competent you are perceived. Yes, it's subjective, but that's the way it is. Life isn't always fair. Sometimes you never get a second chance.

TOGETHERNESS

Togetherness is the inward quality that makes being capable and trustworthy possible. The more together you are, the more organized and "in control" you will be, thus allowing you to better keep your word and do things right. I could spend an entire chapter on togetherness, but I will focus almost entirely on how togetherness looks to another person. In a word, it looks calm. Graceful, cool, in control, are also good words to describe togetherness. Bottom line: People who are perceived to be "together" are perceived to be more competent. Again, this might or might not be true, but perception is reality. Think about this one: would you feel comfortable with a doctor who appeared alarmed and distressed when dealing with patients? The answer is a big NO. I'm certain you'd go out of your way to avoid a doctor who wasn't together, and travel great distances to find one who was. We want our doctors to be together. We want them to be calm, cool, and collected. This reassures us and makes us feel like we are in competent hands.

Doctors aren't alone. The same dynamic is true for every profession. We want our fire fighters, chefs, teachers, receptionists, bus drivers, and retail clerks to be together as well. It's a sign of competency and one that builds comfort and rapport. If they are together, we feel safe and assured in building a relationship. If they appear frazzled, we become skeptical and cautious. We instinctively and unconsciously avoid people whose lives are always in a state of flux.

Picture this example: You suddenly remember one night after dinner that your boss is expecting you to give a presentation to the staff the next morning. The info was compiled days ago, but then you completely forgot. It wasn't ready to be presented to the staff. In a panic, you call a coworker for assistance. She calmly says she'll be glad to help and is on her way. You're frantically getting things ready and are stressed out thinking that your boss might even fire you for a bad presentation. You're at your wit's end when your help arrives. She calmly walks in and without batting an eye assures you that everything will be all right. There's something about those words and her demeanor that almost immediately relieves your anxiety. You work for a couple hours, get the project completed, and you're forever in her debt.

Let's dissect that scenario. We've all been in similar situations. It's natural to react in panic. Sometimes we're able to pull ourselves "together," and sometimes it takes another person to model it for us. By acting calmly and competently, the coworker in the story was able to connect with her panicked colleague. There's something almost magical about the words, "Everything will be all right." It's a beacon of hope and a sign of ultimate togetherness. We recall a time when we were young when someone much bigger and wiser than us put their arms around us and told us everything would be all right. It's emotional rescue at its finest. The words are magical, and we rest in their togetherness.

The difference between whether it's just hollow words or if it's a sincere belief, however, is completely inward. It's being solution focused, instead of problem focused. Too often we get wrapped up in the crisis at hand, unable to see the forest through the trees. This only serves to grow the problem. By believing everything will be all right and focusing on the solution, we empower ourselves (and others) to get things together. Focusing on the solution always shrinks the problem.

Bottom line: Being competent is reassuring to others. It calms them and draws them closer to you. You click because you know what you're doing, they trust you, and you put them at ease. It's a recipe for a solid connection, both outwardly and inwardly!

Quick Click Tip

Make a vow to yourself right now that you will not spend one more minute dwelling on the problems you might be facing. There's too much of that as it is. Problems are everywhere. The key to clicking is to instead dwell on solutions. Openly admit the problem, and then move on. In every problem lies an opportunity, but you'll only see it when you begin seeking solutions. You'll soon get the reputation as someone whom others can rely on to not only be competent, but also to let them know things will be all right. And that might make you the most popular person on the face of the planet!

11

Contagious Principle #9: Compassion

Rapport and compassion have been joined at the hip since the beginning of time. Show me someone who is caring and compassionate, and I'll show you someone who is easy to like. Webster defines compassion as "fellow-suffering, showing sympathy." I, however, believe it is so much more than that. I agree with the fellow part. Fellow means along side, a collaboration of emotion. It's the suffering part that I think falls short. Compassion certainly would include suffering, but it also includes the full array of sympathetic emotions. It's fellow-empathy, fellow-mercy, fellow-forgiveness, fellow-sensitivity, fellow-dependence, and fellow-concern. *Compassion is emotional fellowship.*

Compassion, of course, has inward and outward qualities. The inward qualities are empathy and forgiveness. The outward qualities are sensitivity, mercy, concern, and dependence. Let's start with the inward quality of empathy.

EMPATHY

The intersection of your emotions and another person's emotions is where you'll find empathy. It's putting yourself in their shoes, and seeing things through their eyes. The outward display of empathy is sensitivity and concern, which I'll write about a bit later. Empathy is inward. It's a feeling, or rather a feeling about another person's feelings. Everyone has some level of empathy already. The question is, how much is there, and does it show?

There are three crucial elements to building empathy. The first I've already mentioned; it's seeing things through another person's eyes. It begins with recognition that there is more than one side to every situation. There's a two-step process that I believe helps develop this quality of seeing things through another person's eyes: identification and openness. Identification is identifying with what another person might be feeling through similar feelings of your own. For example, I know what it's like to grow up without a dad because I did for most of my childhood. I can identify with people who had similar experiences, and I can empathize with them easily.

The second step is for those times when identification is not an option. It's when you haven't had a similar experience. This requires openness—being open to imaging how someone might feel even though you've never felt it. It requires being open to foreign feelings and foreign ways of doing things. When I was younger, I used to have an answer for everything. Things were so black and white. There was my way, or no way. It's funny how the older I get, the more I realize just how stupid I was. There's an old Chinese proverb that says it best, "Too soon old, too late smart!"

In my defense, I really wasn't that stupid. I just lacked empathy. I lacked the element of being able to see things through another's eyes. This takes a little life experience. It's recognizing that no one has all the answers, all the time. It's conceding that someone else might feel something you've never felt or know something you don't. This is the beginning of empathy. You might not always be able to identify with someone, but you can always be open. Once you begin to look at the world from other perspectives, inner empathy will flourish.

The second element of empathy is wonder. Again, wonder. I wrote extensively about this in an earlier chapter, but wonder will help you develop empathy. Developing a sense of wonder and being in awe and amazed at the world around you is the nonhuman form of identification and openness. I've trained myself to look at almost everything and try to see beyond the things the eyes can't see. I wonder about the logic behind TV commercials, print ads, company logos and materials, baseball batting line-ups, Web sites, and voice mail greetings. Everything has a story, and it's fun to wonder about the things that came before.

Just today, on the front page of the Money section of *USA Today* was an article about the declining value of the U.S. dollar. The graphic pictured three quarters, two nickels, and a penny representing the dollar's worth. I wondered why they used two nickels instead of one dime. A dime would have saved a coin and would have taken up less space than two nickels. I tried to put myself in the shoes of the person in charge of layout. Maybe they had room to fill and wanted to take up more space, but maybe it was because two nickels have more symbolic and emotional meaning. Everyone's heard the expression about having two nickels to rub together. Maybe they were trying to link the images and the expression with the story. The implication might have been that soon the dollar might not be worth two nickels! Maybe, maybe not, but I wondered anyway. My sense of wonder caused me to empathize with the designers of that article. Wonder will do that. It's a wonderful way to live and an even better way to learn to develop empathy.

The third and final element of empathy is suspending judgment. You can't empathize with another person when you're holding trial on them internally. Unfortunately, we live in an age where everyone is quick to judge. People are more defensive, and it seems like we're just waiting for someone to screw up so we can run them up the flagpole. Religion, politics, race, and gender are but a few of the items that serve as fuel for the fire. Is it any wonder that clicking is such a rare commodity? Clicking is impossible if either party feels attacked or judged.

Whenever I find myself wanting to judge another person, I try to remember that no one is perfect. That's worth repeating, NO ONE IS PERFECT. You might reason that some imperfections are not as bad as others, and while that might be true, I humbly want to remind you that it's all in the eye of the subject of the imperfection. In other words, it's easy to judge when it's someone else.

Now, this is not to suggest that crime shouldn't be prosecuted or wrongdoing shouldn't be righted. I'm merely suggesting that unless you are a judge, it's best to not convict people lest you be convicted. Remember, there's always another side to every situation. Judging is a double-edged sword, and if you live by the sword, you risk getting cut.

FORGIVENESS

It is better to forgive. I'm tempted to just end it right there. That says it all. It's not only better for the person seeking forgiveness; it's better for the person doing the forgiving as well. It's better mentally, emotionally, physically, spiritually, and relationally. When we don't forgive another person, we can't move on. It becomes an emotional sore that continues to fester and never heal. Forgiveness frees us from the bondages of the past. It's emotionally empowering.

The very best information I've ever heard on the subject of forgiveness comes from Michael Wickett's audiocassette series called, "It's All Within Your Reach." In one of his tapes he talks about the healing and rapport power of acceptance, not just with others, but also with yourself. He says that to relive the past is an energy drain, and if you resist letting go of past events and failures, it will grow. "Whatever you resist does more than persist, it expands." Whatever or whomever might be troubling you, the very best thing you could do is to forgive. When you continue to feel bad about something, the problem grows.

For example, if you feel guilty over being in debt, forgive yourself. If you feel terrible about being overweight, forgive yourself. If you feel shame over something that happened years ago, forgive yourself. If someone cheated you in the past, forgive them. If someone lied to you, forgive them. If someone criticized you, forgive them. It's only when you forgive that you're able to really do something positive about the situation. Forgiveness will allow the positive energy to flow and you will find the inner strength to change your life. Guilt, shame, and regret will only serve to keep you anchored in the past. They are useless emotions. If guilt, blame, and regret could change a situation, I'd be all for it, but they can't. They're irrelevant, so forgive and move on. I'm not saying forget. Learn from mistakes so you don't repeat them, but no more. It's a personal choice.

Probably the single best idea I've ever heard on how to cultivate forgiveness came from the late Dr. William McGrane, who was a pioneer in the study and advancement of self-esteem. Bill McGrane taught a philosophy and phrase for people to memorize and say to themselves whenever they feel wronged or slighted in any way. It goes like this: "Everybody, at every point in their life, does the very best they could, and the only thing they were capable of doing given the prevailing awareness they had at that moment." What an awesome belief! It doesn't say that everyone always chooses the right thing. Sometimes people choose to act in not-so-good ways. What it does say however, is that people act based on what they know and how they feel at that given moment in time. Right or wrong, they did the only thing they could have done given their circumstances.

I love the following paragraph on tolerance and forgiveness taken from *The Big Book of Alcoholics Anonymous*.[1] It sums up this philosophy.

> This was our course. We realized that the people who wronged us were perhaps spiritually sick. Though we did not like their

---

[1] *The Big Book of Alcoholics Anonymous*, New York: AA World Services Inc., 1976, pp. 66–67.

symptoms and the way these disturbed us, they, like ourselves, were sick too. We asked God to help us show them the same tolerance, pity, and patience that we would cheerfully grant a sick friend. When a person offended, we said to ourselves, "This is a sick man. How can I be helpful to him? God save me from being angry. Thy will be done."

It's always easy to judge in hindsight. Don't do it. Don't judge others, and more importantly, don't judge yourself. Forgive. It's a simple concept, but it has miraculous benefits.

SENSITIVITY

The outward qualities of compassion begin with being sensitive. I don't mean soft and wishy-washy, but rather aware and in tune with your surroundings. Being sensitive is the outward manifestation of empathy. When you're truly empathetic, you're aware of others and their feelings.

It's incredibly easy to only think about us. We get busy, we've got things to do, and our minds often operate on autopilot. This might be commonplace, but it's extremely bad for clicking. When we get into the zone that only thinks about us, rapport is next to impossible. Clicking requires us to be alert and aware of everything around us. See if any of these situations has ever happened to you. Did you ever say something about another person you thought wasn't in the room only to turn around and see that person standing right there? Have you ever accidentally slammed the door in someone's face? Have you ever done something thinking you were alone and then realized others were watching? Have you ever unwittingly made a derogatory remark? You've probably answered YES to at least one of those questions. While one could chalk it up to bad timing, the case could also be made for lack of awareness. Lack of awareness and sensitivity is almost always a contagion killer.

Unfortunately, there's no magic formula or phrase to develop sensitivity. It simply takes commitment and practice. Make a habit of surveying your surroundings more often and being a little less quick to speak. Sensitivity is almost always nonpassive. In other words, we are most often insensitive by the things we do and say, rather than by the things we didn't do or say. So it stands to reason that the best defense against sensitivity is less offense. By taking the extra second to pause before you speak or act, you will greatly decrease your odds of being insensitive.

MERCY

Mercy is the outward partner to forgiveness. When you forgive some-one, the end result is mercy. Mercy is forgiveness in action. You might forgive someone internally, but it's an act of mercy that lets the other person know about it. Forgiveness without mercy is like a kindness without a gesture.

I have three children, and they have an unwritten code between them. When one does wrong against another, I've never seen any of them ask for forgiveness. Nor have I witnessed any of them verbally forgiving the other. I have, however, witnessed mercy. Just recently one of my kids tattled on another. This was commonplace when they were younger, but it seems the older they get, the less I can count on inside information. My son was furious at his younger sibling for sid-ing with the enemy, the parents. He vowed to never talk to his brother again. Two hours later, the tension was still high, but my older son called out to his brother and asked him if he wanted to play a video game together. The olive branch had been extended. No formal apologies, no requests for forgiveness, just a simple act of mercy.

This is how it is with mercy. It's a subtle gesture that speaks vol-umes. Rapport is very much like that. It's the small things that some-times get overlooked but are instrumental in clicking. Mercy is the olive branch of rapport. It restores broken connections and often even strengthens them.

Many people mistakenly perceive mercy as a weakness, but it's the ultimate act of strength. There's something magical about being the first person to extend mercy. Once mercy is extended, egos can be put aside, the problem resolved, and the relationship restored.

CONCERN

Concern, like mercy, is best displayed through an act. The difference is that mercy needs a wrongdoing; Concern can take place any time, anywhere. Concern is so synonymous with compassion, I almost labeled it a contagion by itself. I decided, however, that concern is an expression of compassion. Concern is to rapport what a smile is to happiness. You can be happy without smiling, but why not smile? You can build rapport with someone without ever having to show any true concern, but why not display your concern? Many relationships begin with an act of concern.

I had just moved to South Carolina a week before I signed up to play for my church's softball team. I had played softball for many years in Northern Virginia and missed the old team immensely, and I still liked the game and wanted to play. They had been playing together for years themselves and I was the newcomer. It was just the second game when I made my mark. I was standing between innings near the first base line as the other team was warming up when suddenly an errant throw struck me on the corner of my eye. Blood squirted everywhere. It was quite a scene.

One of the guys offered to leave the game (which was no small sacrifice) and take me to the emergency room for stitches. He waited with me for more than two hours until I was released to take me home. I was humbled at his concern and compassion. When we pulled up to my house near midnight, my wife was waiting for me, as another team member had alerted her. She wasn't alone. Almost every member of the team was also there to greet me! I barely knew these guys. It was a work night and they had families of their own. I was speechless, and for a professional speaker, this is no small feat. They showed their compassion for a fellow teammate with their concern, and it was a gesture I'll never forget.

Genuine concern is not only a nice, warm, compassionate gesture; it's also a great relational strategy. If there is someone you want to build better rapport with, there's no better way to do it than by displaying thought and concern. A well-timed phone call just to say hello and see how someone is doing, a card or note letting someone know you were thinking about them, remembering little things they tell you as well as the names of their children, and taking someone to dinner when they're sick are excellent examples of concern and compassion.

Concern is even rarer in business. When was the last time someone you do business with called you just to see how you were doing? No strings attached. No ulterior motives. My guess is that it's been a while. The businesses that are good at showing their appreciation and concern for their customers are the businesses that will continue to thrive. The speed of business will continue to increase, but the speed of relationships will always stay the same. It takes time, effort, and concern.

When you get right down to it, concern is nothing more than caring for your fellow friend. When you care about someone, you show concern. Not just when things go bad, but all the time. Showing concern only when it's convenient or when it benefits you is really not genuine concern, and like all faked contagions will be exposed for what it is. Concern originates in the heart, not the head, and the difference is always obvious.

DEPENDENCE

I know that dependence sometimes has negative connotations, but in clicking, dependence is a good thing. We live in a world where independence is celebrated, and we're taught at a very early age not to rely on others for anything. The "do it yourself" mentality is common, and dependence is often viewed as a weakness or even character flaw.

This viewpoint is one of the biggest contributing factors in why clicking is so hard these days. While independence is good in some areas, clicking requires a certain level of dependence on others. Dependence is NOT need. There's a big difference between needing someone and depending on someone.

We depend on people all the time. We depend on other drivers' complying with the law whenever we get behind the wheel. We depend on politicians, airline pilots, coworkers, doctors, farmers, bank tellers, firefighters, policemen, and customers. Dependence is a daily occurrence. Have you ever stopped to thank someone whose dependence you've been taking for granted? Recognizing that we depend on other people all the time is a true sign of compassion and goes a long way in contributing to rapport. Simple acknowledgments are sometimes all that's needed to spark a relationship. A "thumbs up," a smile, a wave, a pat on the back, or a thank you sends a compassionate message that you acknowledge their role in your life.

I give a "thumbs up" every morning to the traffic control person at my son's school. I am dependent on him every morning to get out of the drop-off line and back into the flow of traffic. He always waves back and I never have to wait. I don't know that he treats me any different than any other driver, but I know he'd recognize me if ever I met him elsewhere. We have rapport. If only for a few fleeting seconds a day, I acknowledge my dependence on him, and we click!

In addition to recognizing and acknowledging dependence, we should seek it. I've taught for years that there is a magic phrase for getting people to do something for you. It's quite simple, and I'm sure you've employed it yourself. It's asking for help. "Will you help me?" is probably the single most persuasive question you can ask another person. There's something irresistible in that question. I don't know that I can explain it exactly, but its roots lie in people's deep desire to be needed. We all like to be needed. Sometimes we might think that we're needed too much, but the alternative is worse. I don't have any research for this or scientific data, but I believe that people who are ultra independent have a harder time clicking than those who aren't. My only evidence of this is a few bachelor friends of mine. The older they get, the harder it becomes for them to depend on another person. They become more self-contained with each passing year and admit readily that finding someone who can put up with their independence becomes tougher and tougher.

Conversely, you should look for opportunities to help others. A helping hand is a surefire way to click. The key is twofold. First, don't help expecting something in return. Expecting something in return only makes the other person feel obligated (which isn't always bad) to return the favor. Helping then becomes a strategy. Helping with no strings attached, however, is compassion. Second, don't ask, just do it. It never fails; whenever I ask if someone needs my help, almost always they say, "No, but thanks." What they really meant was, "Yes, but I don't want to be a bother." A much stronger statement would be to not ask, just do. Say, "I'd love to help you," or "Let me give you a hand." Asking might earn you a clicking point or two, but helping without asking will earn you a lot more!

Never hesitate to ask for help, and in turn, never miss an opportunity to help someone else. Helping others is what connects people. I'm thankful and awed, but never surprised at the generous outpouring of compassion that occurs whenever our country is hit with a tragedy. The stories of help and sacrifice with strangers helping strangers could fill an entire library and then some. Compassion is part of the human soul. Sometimes, it just takes a little nudging.

Quick Click Tip

Don't pass up an opportunity to acknowledge another person's contribution to your daily life. Thanking another person and showing gratitude always goes a long way. Also, make a list of all the people who have harmed, hurt, or wronged you in any way. It might take a while, but write down every single name that applies. Then, one by one, forgive each one and cross off their name. You might not forget, but from this moment on, they are forgiven. It's a wonderful act of compassion, and besides, it's highly therapeutic!

12

Contagious Principle #10:
Contentment

Although the contagions are in no particular order, I did save what I believe is the most rare contagion for last: contentment. Everyone wants more than what they've got. We need bigger houses, nicer cars, finer clothes, costlier vacations, and still it's not enough. I know that an argument can be made here that lack of contentment is capitalism at its finest, and that striving for a better lot in life has made this country great.

It's a good argument, and I am in no way talking about complacency. We should strive to be better people and enjoy the fruits of our successes. The difference is twofold. First, I believe the goal should be to be a better person, not to acquire things. When material wealth is our only goal, the victory is usually a hollow one. People have been trying in vain to find happiness in things since the beginning of time. Material possessions should be the fruit of success, not the success itself. Second, we should enjoy the journey and be more appreciative of what we have rather than what we don't have. Striving is good, but when we become so stressed out because we're not where we want to be, then it's time to get off the treadmill.

Contentment breeds peace, and that's something everyone wants. That's what makes it so powerful as a contagion. Everyone seeks it, few find it, but it's out there. There's something tremendously attractive about someone who is content and at peace. There are two outward and two inward qualities that contribute to contentment. The outward are gratitude and enjoyment, and the inward are acceptance and serenity. The outward appear active and the inward appear passive, but they're actually not. Acceptance and serenity can be as powerfully proactive as any quality in this book. Hopefully, you'll agree.

GRATITUDE

Gratitude is appreciation. It's being thankful for what you have. It's both an inward and outward quality. If you're like most people, you've spent 10 times more time feeling bad about what you don't have than feeling appreciative for what you do have. Stop and take inventory. Do you live in a free country? Do you have a roof over your head? Do you have enough food to survive? Do you have any family and friends that care about you? Do you have two working arms and legs? My guess is that you've answered YES to most of those questions, but even if you haven't, there are tons to be grateful for.

The problem is comparison. We see others with perhaps more freedom, a bigger roof, more food, more friends, and better health and we want what they have. Comparison is a trap! It snares you into a never-ending cycle of discontent and stress. It's a game you can't win. It's like the old movie *War Games* with the machine that played a global game of tic-tac-toe. If you play with someone who knows how to play, no one ever wins. The same is true with comparison. No matter how much you have, there is one thing I'll guarantee: there will always be someone else who has more!

One of the most monumental days of life occurred in 1995 in a hotel restaurant in Minneapolis. I had been speaking for almost

10 years at that point and had achieved a level of success most speakers never make. I was one of the youngest speakers to earn the CSP designation. It stands for Certified Speaking Professional, and is given by the National Speakers Association. My first book was due out later that year and I had a family who loved me. By all accounts, I should have been on cloud nine, but I wasn't. I was frustrated. I had planned on being much further along in my career after 10 years than I was. Some of my peers, many who had been speaking for less time than me, appeared much better off than I was. I was working 60 hours a week and had trouble sleeping. I was racing against time. Someone told me that I could sleep when I'm dead, that I must seize the moment and achieve all I could, when I could. I was physically, emotionally, financially, and spiritually exhausted.

I was having lunch with Glenna Salsbury, (remember her?),a Hall of Fame speaker whom I had admired from the day I became a speaker. If you had asked me at the time why I admired her, I would have cited her many professional accomplishments, but my reasons now would be much different. About halfway through lunch, she stopped and looked me squarely in the eyes and asked me perhaps the most penetrating question I've ever been asked. "If I never achieve anything more than what I've already achieved, would that be good enough for me?" I hesitated, but my insides were screaming, "NO WAY." I was after greatness and anything short of that would be unacceptable. I wondered why she would ask me such a question. Was she testing me? Is there a right or wrong answer? My mind was spinning and I finally responded with a definitive, "I don't know."

That kind of summed up where I was. I didn't know. She gently proceeded to tell me that until we are grateful for what we have, we would never have anything more. "Surely," I thought, "there were ungrateful people with a lot more than me. What did she mean by that?" She never elaborated, but I've since figured it out for myself. Certainly, an ungrateful person can have more things. The "more" she was talking about wasn't things. It was peace and happiness. Unless we are grateful for what we have, we'll never be happy with more.

If we don't learn to be grateful, we'll never break that cycle of discontent and stress.

We should live with inner appreciation and outer gratitude. We should be thankful for each day and exhibit that gratitude for others to see. The most persuasive people I know are also the most grateful. It's not a coincidence. Gratitude is contagious!

ENJOYMENT

When we feel grateful and begin to show it, we must constantly remind ourselves to enjoy the journey and live in the present. It's great to have a vision, in fact I wrote about that in Chapter 6, but we should enjoy each step along the way. Enjoyment is a fruit of gratitude. You can't enjoy until you're thankful. Once you're thankful, then you're ready for real enjoyment. When was the last time you ever said you enjoyed having a roof over your head? Or that you enjoyed your job? Or enjoyed your health? Being grateful is only half the equation; you must also enjoy the things you are thankful for. Don't take anything for granted. Enjoy the rain, as well as the sun. Enjoy the challenging times, as well as the victories. Enjoy your kids; they too soon will be adults. Enjoy being sick; it might be your body telling you to slow down. Enjoy the scenery of life. Enjoy trees, bushes, birds, dogs, rivers, thunderstorms, and rainbows. Enjoy them now. Tomorrow is not guaranteed for any of us.

The biggest hurdle to enjoyment is something I call "when" disease. "When" disease is a condition characterized by an overdependence on a future event. For example, complete this sentence: "I'll be happy WHEN I _____. That is "when" disease. I'll be happy when, or satisfied when, or take a vacation when, or spend time with my kids when, or do volunteer work when. It's a disease that is very hard to get rid of. The only way to slowly rid yourself of this disease is to substitute the word NOW for when. Every time your mind wants to play the "when" game, you can override your thinking by verbally saying NOW. Saying things out loud is the only way to change your thinking. It might take a few times, but slowly and surely, you can eradicate "when" disease. Be happy NOW. Be satisfied NOW. Be grateful NOW.

ACCEPTANCE

The inner journey to contentment begins and ends with acceptance. In fact, you'll have a hard time being grateful and enjoying life if you don't accept your lot in life. Again, it's important to note that I am not advocating complacency or giving up. Acceptance is entirely internal. Acceptance can only be shown through the external qualities of gratefulness and enjoyment. Gratitude is your being grateful and displaying thankfulness for something outside yourself. Enjoyment is your enjoying your physical journey and the world around you. Acceptance is your being OK with you. It's completely inward. It's accepting the things you cannot change.

You've heard the old saying about having the power to change the things you can and to accept the things you can't, and the wisdom to know the difference. That's what I'm talking about. Absolutely, change the things you can. Strive to be better, but accept the things that are outside your control. On the external front, for example, there's no use in yelling at the weather; you can't do anything about it. More importantly, on the internal front, you must accept certain things as well. I'll never run as fast as I used to. I'll never be a professional baseball player. Maybe there was a time when I could, but not anymore. No amount of wishing and practice will make it happen. I'll never be 20 again. I'll never be a girl.[1] I'll never discover the cure for polio. That's already been done. These things are impossible due to physical limitations. However, there are other limitations that I must accept as well. I will never be president of the

---

[1] OK. I could undergo a gender change, but all that will do is change the outside. Some people elect this procedure so that their outside matches their inside. This is not the case for me, so the best thing I can do is accept it.

United States. This is not because it is physically impossible to do, but rather because it is emotionally impossible. To be president, I'd first have to WANT to be president, and I don't want to. At least not right now. I might have a change of heart, but that's another thing I can't control: how I'll feel in the future.

The point is you should accept your physical and emotional limitations. They are uniquely yours. Accepting the things you cannot change and being content with them have amazingly contagious effects.

When I was a teenager I worked as a home health aide. It's an unusual job for a teenage boy to have, but I didn't like working at McDonalds, and my job with HomeCall afforded me flexible hours and better pay. My first and longest case (I had it for three years) was to care for a young man named Mike Parsley.

Mike is one of, if not the, most incredible people I have ever met. Mike was 32 when I met him. He was in an automobile accident a year earlier that left him a quadriplegic. His wife left him and took two of his three children with her. He was left with no job and no money and was forced to move back into the living room of his elderly parent's tiny, run-down apartment. His oldest son, a 12-year-old, elected to live with him. My first instinct was to feel sorry for him, but he never let me. From the very first day I met him, he had accepted his situation and was at total peace. He was the happiest person I knew. With all the tact of a 17-year-old, I'd ask him if he was bitter, and I can still close my eyes and hear him reply, "What's there to be bitter about?" I remember thinking, "Everything!"

But he proclaimed his gratitude for his parents, a roof over his head, his children, God, and me. I'd walk in, usually running late and in a panic, and his first order of business was to dispatch me to the window to find a bird that had been singing to him all morning. He told me at least 100 times in the three years I cared for him that he couldn't go back and change what happened, so he might as well accept it and make the best out of it. "I can't control what's done, but I can control my reaction, moods, and thoughts," he used to say. I don't know that I understood, nor did I realize it at the time, but the lessons he taught me were more important than any formal education I could have gotten. It sure beat flipping burgers!

I've often thought about Mike Parsley through the years. I've tried to find him several times with no luck. I haven't even found a thread of evidence that he even existed. The old apartment building is still standing but has changed tenants a dozen times. I can't find record of his parents, and I'm sure they've long since passed away. I never met his ex-wife and can't remember the names of any of his children. Name searches on the Internet have come up empty. It's even crossed my mind that he was an angel or figment of my imagination. Whatever he was, he was amazing. I wish I could thank him personally some day!

SERENITY

Probably the biggest lesson Mike had ever taught me was the same one that was later echoed by Glenna. Serenity is contagious. It's a sense of calmness, peace, and that everything will work out the way it was meant to be. The foundation of serenity is a belief in something bigger and more powerful than we are. For me, as it is with Mike Parsley and Glenna Salsbury, it's not a something, it's a someone. For us He's God, but whomever you might call on, the day that we surrender to something bigger than ourselves is the day we can begin to find true contentment and peace. I couldn't begin to think about clicking with others unless I knew God was in charge of the outcomes. It gives me serenity, peace. I do my best and surrender the results to Him. It gets my ego out of the way and allows me to sleep better at nights. It means that not only do I accept the things I cannot control, but I'm also calm and reassured when bad or unexpected things happen. It isn't all about me.

Some people never wake up to the fact that they aren't the center of the universe and that there are some things out of their control. They need to control and explain everything. They are the classic control freaks. They can be dangerous because they haven't figured out which things are controllable and which are not. Surrender is not in their vocabulary. Unfortunately, they rarely find peace. Most people only discover serenity after failure upon failure. When doing things their way don't produce the results and happiness they are looking for, only then do people look to surrender to a higher force. I believe the earlier the better.

The contagious part, however, is not the higher force; it's the peace and serenity that goes along with it. This serenity allows you to recognize God at work and enjoy the adventure with Him. Too many people aren't enjoying the adventure. People won't be willing to join you if you're not having fun.

I had to surrender to the fact that God knows what's best for me, even if I don't understand all that might be happening around me. I don't have to understand; I just need to accept and be thankful. It's not always easy to do, especially when things don't go your way. I know it sounds like a Rolling Stones song, but it's an incredible truth: You don't always get what you want, but you always get what you need. My life is a living testimony to that.

I was born David Maiatico, (pronounced Me-ah-tiko), a good Italian name, in Allentown, Pennsylvania. Thanks to Billy Joel, most people know where that is. My mother and father divorced when I was three and my sister and I grew up without a dad. I guess you could say we grew up lower middle class, but that was only because of my grandparents, who moved in and helped out. My mother took the best job she could find, a bookkeeper at Howard Johnson's. Needless to say, money was tight. In fact, money seemed to be the only argument that ever took place in our house. I remember one fight in particular involved baseball. I love baseball and always have. As much as I love speaking and consulting, if the Dodgers called me today and asked me to play for them, I'd go in a skinny minute.[2] I can't recall the argument specifics, but I do know that I only played one year of organized

---

[2]That's southern for "really fast."

baseball because we just couldn't afford it. Besides, because my mother worked a lot at night, I'd have no way to get to and from games and practices. I made up for it by playing more than my share of baseball in the neighborhood. Our daily games have become legendary in our minds, but I still have my South Allentown Optimists baseball cap from that year I played.

Fighting over money, or should I say lack thereof, seemed like a daily ritual and I took refuge behind the shed in our back yard. There was a three-foot gap between the back of the shed and our fence, and that became my safe haven when the fighting got too intense.

I said a prayer that I must have said dozens, if not hundreds, of times. It went something like this: "Dear God, I don't care how you do it, but I want to be rich when I grow up!" I certainly didn't know then the secrets of contentment. I wanted to be rich, and that was all there was to it.

Well, let me fast forward the story a bit. When I was 12, my mother remarried and the man she married adopted my 10-year-old sister and me. When that happens, you are issued a new birth certificate reflecting your new last name. His last name was Rich, and overnight, I became Rich.

I often say the moral of my story is that when making requests of God, you need to be very specific. Apparently, I wasn't specific enough, but the real moral of the story is that although I didn't get the monetary gains I prayed for, I got exactly what I needed. I got something better and more valuable than money, and that was a dad. To borrow a line from Garth Brooks, "Some of God's greatest gifts are unanswered prayers."

The events that led to my mother getting married again were completely out of my control, but they weren't out of God's. Serenity comes from the secure belief that things happen for a reason. I might not have realized it at the time, but I've found peace in knowing that someone bigger than me was in control.

I continue to talk to God and set goals, and I have a vision for the rest of my life. I strive for the best, but I'm content with the results

" But if not I'm still going to be happy "

and the journey along the way. I have adopted three little words that help me stay content and peaceful. The words: "But if not." Sure I have big plans for my future, *but if not*, I'm still going to be happy. I pray for health and a long life, *but if not,* I'm still going to enjoy what I have. I'd love for everyone to love this book, *but if not*, it's been a wonderful experience for me. *"But if not"* is the key to serenity. Some might say it's a cop-out, but I call it life.

Erma Bombeck once wrote the following paragraph in a column titled, "If I Had My Life to Live Over Again:"

> I would have invited friends over to dinner even if the carpet was stained and the sofa faded. I would have sat on the lawn with my children and not worried about grass stains. I would never have bought anything just because it was practical, wouldn't show soil, or was guaranteed to last a lifetime. When my child kissed me impetuously, I would never have said, "Later, now get washed up for dinner." There would have been more "I love you's," more "I'm sorry's," but mostly, given another shot at life, I would seize every minute, look at it and really see it, live it, and never give it back.

Live each day to the fullest and when it's over, smile and be content. Others will find that irresistible, and you'll find peace.

Quick Click Tip

Go somewhere where you can be alone for a few minutes. Close your eyes. Sit still. Just be. Breathe deeply. Relax. There's no one to impress, and no one is watching. It's just you and your thoughts. Have a little talk with yourself. Confess your worries, and express your gratitude. Enjoy the quiet. You might be restless and impatient at first, but stick with it. If you can learn to be content with yourself, doing absolutely nothing, the rest is easy. Do this once a day for at least five minutes. The stillness can be most powerful.

13

Putting It All Together: Congruency

So, there are a couple of burning unanswered questions at this point: Do you need to master all 10 contagions to click? And can you fake your way through any of the contagions that you haven't mastered? Let's start with the first one.

I concede that the thought of having to master all the aspects of 10 different contagions every time you want to click with someone has probably left you a bit overwhelmed. Well, take a deep breath; it's not that daunting a task. Clicking might be the sum of the parts, but not all parts are necessary to create a solid rapport. Different contagions are needed for different situations and different kinds of people. Someone might really admire confidence, while another is looking for contentment. You sometimes never know what contagions clicked and which ones you might have lacked.

Clicking is something you never fully master. Striving to click with everyone every time is a worthy endeavor and one where even if you fall short, you still win. The magical secret about aspiring to click is that it's a win-win. The obvious win is the improvement in the quantity and quality of your relationships. I'd be willing to bet that was your motivation in buying this book.

However, there's a secondary benefit which will pay you dividends down the road, and that's the change in you. The person you'll become is a far greater reward than any single earthly relationship you might have. In your quest to click with others, you'll come to realize that clicking first begins with you. I've said repeatedly that you won't click with others until you first click with yourself. Clicking originates inside and manifests itself outside. In other words, the fruits might be visible in the quantity and quality of your relationships, but it always begins inside. Fellow author and speaker Zig Ziglar is known for saying, "If you help enough other people get what they want, you'll get what you want in the process." That's the way it is with clicking. Your journey to clicking will improve all areas of your life. But don't expect miracles. Clicking takes time.

I love the word clicking because it has multiple meanings. Not only does it mean having rapport with someone, but it's also a wonderful description of the way we learn. Picture a ratchet wrench. If you're as inept as I am with tools, this is no easy feat, but a ratchet wrench works by gradually tightening the nut or bolt. Do I sound like Bob Vila yet? Anyway, as it tightens it makes a clicking sound. Each click is one notch tighter than the click before. That's the way we progress through life as well. One click at a time. Sometimes we make great strides and move several clicks forward.

Hopefully this book has clicked you forward a few notches. Sometimes we stay focused and tightened, but often we lose a click or two if we stay dedicated to the journey. I know my life is filled with times when I moved three clicks forward, then two clicks back. I beat myself up and down for moving backward, failing to recognize that I am one click further than I was before. Change is subtle. Ratchet wrenches make so many clicking sounds it's hard to know when it is tightening and loosening. Relationships, as well as life itself, are the same. It's hard to know when you're moving forward.

We're simply not capable of judging that. Many times I thought I was moving forward only to later learn I wasn't, and vice versa. All you can do is trust your instincts, knowledge, and synchronicity. A tradesman must trust his tools.

In the same vein, it's noble to set out to click with everyone every time, but all you can really control is how well you trust and master the contagions.

As for the question of faking, you can fake certain things inwardly for a while in hopes of affecting the outward, but if that is all it ever is, it will eventually be exposed. In other words, clicking is more an act of being than an act of doing. The conversion from doing to being is congruency. It's the intersection of the inward and outward you. The more natural the contagions are to you, the more congruent you become, the more congruent, the better you become at clicking.

The issue of congruency is small matter. If others don't think our actions or words match the person we really are, then our ability to click is significantly diminished. In a recent poll of more than 1000 American workers, the question was raised whether the actions of the senior leaders at the companies they worked for were consistent with their words.[1] A third of the respondents said NO, and another 12 percent said they weren't sure or would rather not answer.

You cannot fake congruency. You might be able to fool somebody here or there, but never for long, and even more importantly, you'll never fool yourself. Congruency is the ability to look yourself in the mirror every morning and know that what you see is real. It's a huge dilemma for professional speakers and anyone who makes a living in the public eye, but it's no less important for those who don't. We want our leaders, bosses, speakers, sports heroes, and movie stars to be shining examples of congruency, but sadly, that's rarely the case.

---

[1] Marist Poll of 1003 Americans as cited in *USA Today*. Margin of error: 3.1 percentage points.

The more we uncover about them, the less esteem we have for them. That's not the way it should be. Congruency is being the person others think we are. No games, no faking; what you see is what you get.

Congruency is to clicking what threads are to a garment. It seems like a funny analogy, but it works. No one ever notices the threads until there's a tear, and it's the threads that determine the quality of the garment. Congruency works the same way. Congruency determines the quality of the relationship. You might get through an interaction or two with a loose stitch, but eventually, the garment will come apart. Congruency holds the contagions together. It doesn't happen overnight, but it happens click by click until you arrive at the person you want to be.

14

Can a Business Be Contagious?

In a nutshell, yes. There are businesses, like individuals, who are more contagious and are easier to click with. For example, have you ever wondered what it is exactly that makes companies like Starbucks, Southwest, Dell, Microsoft, Wal-Mart, and FedEx among America's most admired?[1] One can argue that it's because they've become household names and that they do a lot of advertising. That's certainly a factor, but so do Sears, McDonalds, United, and Pepsi, but they aren't on the list. Clicking requires more than just a familiar name; it requires that a company be contagious.

The same qualities that allow an individual to click are the same ones necessary for a business. I could make a case for any of the contagions. *Competency* is an obvious given. Competency is more about perception than it is about performance. What a customer believes is as powerful as what a business does. Contagious businesses create and control customer perceptions. A contagious business is a *confident*

---

[1]According to *Fortune* magazine.

business. I can tell almost immediately when I walk into a retail business or speak to someone over the phone whether they are confident by showing pride in what they do. A contagious business also shows *curiosity*, constantly wanting to know and learn more about its customers.

Commitment and *conviction* are also essential. Al Davis, owner of football's Oakland Raiders preached "commitment to excellence" and coined the slogan, "Just win, baby!" *Contentment* is also important. Success dooms more businesses than failure. Greed leads to biting off more than it can chew, which in turn compromises quality and reputation. It's the other four contagions that I will focus on in this chapter: *Cheerfulness, Connectedness, Compassion*, and *Courage*.

CHEERFULNESS

OK, a business needs to be cheerful, but it's a bit more complex than that. Sure, everyone that even has a smidgeon of customer contact must be pleasant and cheerful, but it's not enough just to be nice. The customer must be able to FEEL the cheerfulness in order for it to be truly contagious. There's a bit of a difference there.

I've dealt with many businesses where they were properly trained to act cheerful, but very few are educated as to how to translate that cheerfulness to a customer. I wrote about the difference between training and education in Chapter 1, but the subtle difference between the two is at the heart of contagiousness. Training tells someone what to do, how to do it, and even when to do it. Education tells them *why* to do it.

Most customer service departments and telemarketing operations have at some time or another tried putting mirrors at workers' desks so that they can see themselves while they are on the phone and remember to smile. They're quick to point out that a smile can be heard over the telephone, and some companies have even mandated it as company policy. What they fail to teach, however, is *why* greeting a customer with a smile is so crucial. The answer is a simple one.

People *want* to do business with people who are cheerful and love what they do. A smile sets the tone for the entire interaction.

I will go out of my way to do business with people who are cheerful. I'm even willing to pay more. Cheerfulness is that important to me. To me, it's a very conscious thing. For others, it might not be as conscious. Cheerfulness, or lack of it, is often a silent, but deadly, business killer.

Let's face it, customers, or prospective customers, will not confess that the reason they've chosen not to do business with you is because they just didn't like you or your attitude. Nine out of ten times two people choose not to do business together is because of lack of rapport regardless of what they might say. It's embarrassing and awkward for someone to admit a clicking problem. Instead, they'll cite the more palpable excuses of price, budget, and timing. They'll say they've decided to hold off on a purchase rather than admitting it was because of your attitude and lack of cheerfulness, or in the case of retail, they simply wouldn't come back.

Cheerfulness can and should be a priority for any business. To do so, two things are essential. First, a business must eliminate all negativity. Negativity is a cancer that grows from within, sometimes undetected until it's too late. Schools and public institutions have declared their war on drugs by establishing "drug-free" zones, so too a business should fight negativity head-on by declaring their business a "negative-free" zone. Gather around the water cooler if you must, but complaining and whining will not be part of the banter. A worker who is productive, but negative is, in my book, unproductive and should be let go. That might sound harsh, but business in the twenty-first century is fierce and unforgiving. Customers want to do business with companies that promote positiveness and leave them feeling uplifted. Today's employees want more than a paycheck. They want meaningful work; above all, they want to have fun.

Fun is the second ingredient in creating a cheerful business. Show me a company where everyone has fun and I'll show you a contagious business. A company that has fun also is more productive.

I know of a few companies that are serious and committed to having fun. One company has taken the mirror concept one step further by mandating a 3-to-5-second laugh before answering the phone. It's an amazing (and contagious) thing to watch. Phones are ringing throughout the department, but before picking up, the person laughs for a few seconds. At first, the laughs are less than sincere, but it doesn't take long before it turns sincere. New employees report sore facial muscles after the first day or two before getting used to it. The days go by quicker, they feel less stress, and they even have customers who call simply for a pick-me-up. Another company I've run across has what they call, "Fun Time Outs." Once in midmorning and once in midafternoon, small teams gather for 10 minutes of fellowship, laughter, and joke telling. They hand out prizes for the best joke of the day. In short, they make having fun a priority, and the results are unmistakable. They have less turnover, less stress, are more productive, have greater camaraderie, and this all adds up to happier and more loyal customers.

CONNECTEDNESS

Unlike personal connectedness, a business must connect in more abstract ways. In addition to connecting with customers one by one, a business must connect with customers as a whole. It's a lot like public speaking. When I'm speaking in front of hundreds of people, I can't single one person out and solely connect with that person. I'd risk alienating the rest of the audience. I must connect with the group as a whole. This is the difference between personal and organizational contagiousness. Organizational clicking can, like personal clicking, happen in an instant, but more often than not, it takes a bit more time. Connectedness in business has three ingredients: desire, patience, and consistency. It goes without saying that a business first must have the desire to connect.

Connections that are made by accident rarely last beyond the transaction at hand. It amazes me how many businesses I come into contact with that don't seem to have any desire or game plan to connect with their customers, but then act surprised when customers aren't loyal. All clicking starts with a sincere desire to do so.

Then comes the hard part: patience. Businesses want to skip the effort part and proceed directly to the bottom line. Your best friends aren't your best friends because both parties entered into a friendship agreement. You're best friends because of history. You're best friends because of blood, sweat, and tears, and because you've built a relationship over time. Same is true with businesses. You won't have a loyal customer simply because you've entered some agreement and contracts have been signed.

Loyalty takes effort, and it takes time. Probably the single biggest mistake businesses make is that their focus has become making money today instead of building a business for tomorrow. Businesses cannot survive without customers, and loyal customers are better than disloyal ones. You build a business one relationship at a time. There's a big difference between a customer and a client. A customer is someone who has bought from you; a client is someone who will buy from you. One step further, however, is a supporter. A supporter is someone who will not only continue to buy from you, but will spread the word, singing your praises. They support you every chance they get. Thus the goal should be not to simply gain a customer, but to gain a supporter. That takes time. From the other point of view, a customer might see you only as a vendor, but a supporter will see you as a valued resource and even as a friend.

I often say in my seminars, you don't grow a business, you grow your people, and as a result of your people growing, your business grows. Well, to put a different spin on that, you don't build a business, you build relationships, and as a result of building relationships, you build a business.

A business also needs to be consistent. Consistency is so important that I toyed with the idea of including it as its own contagion. Any business can be cheerful and pleasant at any given moment, but contagious businesses are cheerful and pleasant at all moments. I scratch my head sometimes at the amount of money and hoopla some businesses go through each October during National Customer Service Week. It's usually the first week of October and some businesses go all out. I can appreciate that. The part that baffles me is that many businesses think this is the time to show appreciation for their customers, and when the week is up, they revert back to taking customers for granted. It's wonderful to celebrate that week, but showing appreciation should happen all year long.

Consistency in customer service will connect, but sporadic razzle-dazzle will be seen for what it is: fake and too late. Businesses can and should be ready to make changes on a dime, but the one thing that should never change is their commitment to connect. Consistency wins the race every time.

COMPASSION

I can sum up this segment with just one question: Do you really care about your customers? I believe most businesses would say "yes," but I believe it's a qualified "yes." It's easy to care when all is going well. When all the bills are paid, the phones are fairly quiet, and there's peace within the walls, then it's easy to care. It's a whole other ball game when reality strikes. Let me change the question a bit: Do you still care and are able to show it when the phones are ringing off the hook and your company is struggling?

Compassion is easy when all is well, but your ability to click as a business increases a hundredfold if you're compassionate when things are hectic.

Whenever I sign on a new client, one of the standard practices is to give me a tour of their operations. I truly love to see how different businesses are run, but I don't like prearranged tours. I prefer to pop in. I want to see things as they are every day, when they're not expecting company. That's when I can best gauge their compassion level.

The signs of a contagiously compassionate company are evident when one first walks in the door. Here's a partial checklist of 10 questions:

1. Is there an immediate greeting?
2. Is it warm and sincere?
3. Do people say "hello" to each other and newcomers in the hallways?
4. Are visitors issued a name badge?
5. Are people smiling?
6. Are people anxious to answer the phone?
7. Is there a toll-free phone number for customers?
8. Is there a dedicated customer service function?
9. Does everyone sound upbeat and positive?
10. Do the customer service reps appear to be sincere in handling customer concerns?

These are just a few of the things I look for to determine compassion. Compassion is much more subjective than objective, but one can feel its presence. If I can, so can customers? Let me zero in on a couple of the questions above.

First, is there an immediate greeting? The first sign of a compassionate company is an urgency to greet visitors. Contagiously compassionate companies treat visitors like guests in their homes. Second, how do the employees interact when walking through the hallways? It's hard to care about customers if you don't care about each other.

Compassionate companies are companies where people feel free and encouraged to smile, shake hands, and give a "thumbs up" to coworkers when passing by. On the other extreme, uncontagious companies breed employees who walk with their heads down and rarely acknowledge each other, let alone a visitor. Unfortunately, I've even run across a few companies that flat out tell employees NOT to say "hello" to visitors. I can only guess at the twisted logic that was involved in that decision.

Lastly, is a customer service a priority? Lots of companies give wonderful lip service to customer service, but when it comes right down to it, there's not much there. Customer service is the lifeblood of any business. It should be something that is overt and central to any business. It's more than a department or job title; it's an ethic that runs from top to bottom. Contagious companies instinctively understand this, while many others can't seem to grasp the concept.

I was wandering through the hallway one time of a well-known Fortune 500 company when I overheard what might be the dumbest remark I've heard in business. I heard a customer service rep say that she "could get a whole lot more work done if only customers would stop bugging her." It stopped me dead in my tracks, but upon further thought, it shouldn't have surprised me. To her, the customer only meant more work. She knows her job is to deal with customers, but she lacks the compassion for doing so. Contagiousness demands compassion. In business, it's not a luxury; it's a necessity. If a company expects to succeed in these ultracompetitive times, the customer better represent more than just a necessary evil.

COURAGE

Business can be scary. Things change in the blink of any eye. Businesses that were on top of the world one day might be fighting for survival the next. Consider how things have changed over the past 100 years.

One hundred years ago, the average life expectancy was only 47. Only 14 percent of homes had a bathtub, and only 8 percent had a telephone. The average wage was 22 cents per hour, and only 6 percent of the population graduated from high school. Iowa, Tennessee, and Mississippi were more populated than California, and the population of Las Vegas was 30! Crossword puzzles, canned beer, and iced tea had not been invented yet. Drug stores advertised heroin as being "good for the complexion." The leading causes of death were pneumonia, tuberculosis, and diarrhea. Hard to imagine, isn't it?

The point is, 100 years from now, they'll be looking back with the same amazement at how things have changed. Possibilities are endless. Ideas can change the world. The catch is to act on your idea, and that takes courage. It takes courage to step out from behind the safety of security and take a chance. It takes courage to try something that is completely foreign and unknown to you. It takes courage to be different. It takes courage to begin.

I'll start with beginning. Beginning is the hardest part of action. Lots of great ideas never see the light of day because someone lacked the courage to begin. It's OK to start small. You'd be in good company. Michael Dell, of Dell Computers, sold computer parts from a college dorm room. Today his company sells more than 7 billion dollars worth of computers and accessories. Philip Knight, founder of Nike, sold imported Japanese sneakers from the back of his station wagon. The Gallo brothers, founders of E & J Gallo Winery, started by studying wine making at night in their local library. They may have all had humble beginnings, but they also had the courage to act on their convictions. They were willing to take a chance. Businesses start every day, yet very few make it as big as Dell or Nike. What's their secret? Well, that answer is a book in itself, but part of that answer is that they dared to be different. They offered something unique, something that no one else was doing. The courage to be different is the absolute key to business success. There are three ways for a business to be different. They can be different through invention, re-invention, and promotion.

Invention is simple. This is inventing a new product or service. This is coming up with a new mousetrap. It happens every day. Record numbers of submissions are sent to the United States Trademark and Patent Office each month. All it takes is a little possibility thinking. Creativity is the child of courage. A business that stops innovating is a dying business. In my opinion, it's as simplistic as innovate or die.

Re-invention is kind of like invention, only it's not coming up with a new mousetrap, but a different spin on the old mousetrap. That makes it new again. One of my favorite examples of re-invention is the story of Richard Heinichen. He bottles and sells rainwater. He calls it "fresh squeezed cloud juice." It might sound nutty, but as of this printing, two supermarkets had agreed to carry it and there are calls from dozens more. He hopes to franchise the rainwater-bottling concept very soon! He didn't invent rainwater. I'm sure he's not the first to bottle it, but as far as I know, he's the first to have the gumption to sell it! You might be thinking, "I've thought of that," and you might have. Only he had the courage to take action.

Re-invention is not exclusively for products. Services can be re-invented as well. Over the past 10 years, I had the privilege of working with dozens of temporary staffing firms. That is one of the many industries in desperate need of re-invention. I say that because the decision to use one staffing firm over another is almost solely based on price. I call it commoditization, and is the telltale sign of an industry that is lacking innovation and needs to be re-invented.

The only way to defeat commoditization is by differentiation. A few of my staffing clients have been courageous and bold enough to re-invent their businesses, and it's paid off. One client has revolutionized its screening and interviewing process. They started referring to their new process as "The Science of Selection," and their profits have risen. Another staffing client has differentiated by establishing a "University" to train and certify workers before going on a job assignment. It's caught on so well that even their competitors have begun using their University!

These are just a few of the countless examples of businesses across the country that have been bold enough to attempt to stand out and re-invent their businesses. They might seem small, but that's OK. Small differences can make a huge difference. Of course, the bolder, the better, or should I say, the bolder, the more contagious!

Promotion is neither being different through invention, nor re-invention, but rather through the means in which you promote and market your business. Coming up with some new twist or spin that is different is sometimes all that's needed.

One of my best friends was once a struggling real estate agent. He loved real estate, but he lived in a big metropolitan city where competition was fierce and plentiful. We were both new in our careers when we gathered one night at our favorite pizza joint. We talked about ways we could stand out and get more business. Almost half joking, I suggested he create a super hero character, called "Real Estate Man." We were both superhero character fans growing up (mine is Underdog), and if there was anyone who could pull it off, it was him. We talked about a costume complete with cape, tights, and a big R across his chest. His logo could be him flying through the air or standing holding up houses with each arm with a tag line that read: "If I can't move your house, it can't be moved!" Instead of a boring monthly or quarterly newsletter,[2] he could put out a comic strip chronicling the adventures of Real Estate Man and how he saved another couple from financial disaster. The more we giggled over the idea, the more I liked it. By evening's end, though, he sadly proclaimed he couldn't do it. He said the real estate industry wasn't ready for a middle-aged man in tights. He said that the new law firm downtown probably wouldn't want its agent to show up in a cape and a Speedo. He'd be the laughing stock of the industry. He passed on the idea, and today he's out of real estate.

Now don't misunderstand my point. He was right in all his assumptions, and there is no guarantee that had he tried the idea he'd still be in real estate. No one knows, but I know it would have been worth the risk. Yes, it is true that his law firm client would probably look elsewhere, and yes, it is true that he'd attract a lot of attention. However, I contend that for every client he lost for being Real Estate Man, there was someone who would choose him because of it. When you're bold, you'll attract a host of people waiting to shoot you down,

---

[2] Boring because it's been done to death.

but only initially. Then people will line up to sing your praises! The little-known truth about business is that whenever you try to be all things to all people, you end up being nothing to nobody. In other words, no matter what you do, some people will not like what you're doing, so why not take a chance? Businesses are drowning in a sea of vanilla, and most are losing the battle. When the game plan becomes not to lose money or customers, the irony is that's exactly what happens.

The question that every business cannot afford not to answer is this: What can you do that will make you unique and stand out? The quicker you answer that and begin to promote that uniqueness, the faster you'll become contagious. I'll end with an anonymous quote that much more succinctly says what I've been trying to say: "Do not follow where the path may lead. Go instead where there is no path and leave a trail."

A Final Thought

Being contagious and clicking with others is at the heart of every transaction and interaction, both outwardly and inwardly. Yet for too many people, rapport is some whimsical phenomenon that sometimes happens and sometimes doesn't. I set out to show that clicking is a deliberate act, and it is a worthy endeavor to set out to click with everyone every time. I hope I've built the case that it is controllable and completely within your power. Rapport is like any other skill. The more you work at it, the better and more natural it becomes. In these fast-paced, competitive times, clicking is not just a luxury; it is an absolute necessity. Because relationships are the crucial to almost every endeavor, the more people you click with, the higher your quality of life will be.

With all that said, however, it hit me that while it might be highly desirable to click with everyone every time, the truth is you won't. Good old-fashioned common sense tells me that as hard as you might try, with some people, you'll clash. There have been many times that I wanted to click with someone so badly and tried my hardest to do so, yet it didn't happen. This is simply a fact of life. As I've stated from the beginning, clicking is highly subjective and personal, and what clicks with one person might have the completely opposite effect on another. At least outwardly. My hope is that the frequency and depth of your outward clicking will increase dramatically as a result of this book, but in the times when it doesn't happen, brush yourself off and stay positive. While you won't click with everyone every time in the outward sense, you can do it every time in the inward sense. It sounds like double speak, but stay with me, we're almost done.

The person you can click with every time is yourself. Clicking is the process by which others come to like you, AND the process in which you come to like yourself. It's the ultimate self-help journey. You click more often outwardly when you click inwardly every time. There might not always be outwardly clicking with others, but there can and should always be an inner clicking with you. It doesn't work the other way around. Clicking inside will change your life outside.

I'll leave you (how else?) with a quote from Ralph Waldo Emerson, "It is one of the most beautiful compensations of this life that no man can sincerely try to help another without helping himself." It happens every time! That's the beauty of clicking. It's the ultimate click!

Good luck.

Index

About the Author

David A. Rich is a nationally recognized speaker and expert in persuasion and motivation. He has presented to over a half million people in 44 states and 4 countries for groups from the Fortune 100 to small community churches.